Gérard (

The

Accursed Treasure

of

Rennes-le-Château

with the collaboration of
SOPHIE DE SÈDE

Translated by Henry Lincoln © 2012

Barbara Levy Literary Agency
64, GREENHILL
HAMPSTEAD HIGH STREET
LONDON NW3 5TZ

Tel: 00 44 20 84 55 13 13
blevy@dircon.co.uk

© 2013 LES ÉDITIONS DE L'ŒIL DU SPHINX
ISBN: 979-10-91506-10-6
EAN: 9791091506106
ISSN of the collection: 1768-5648
Publication registered: August 2013
Graphics and design: www.plaisibook.com

The
Accursed Treasure
of
Rennes-le-Château

Gérard de Sède

Collection Serpent Rouge n°33

FOREWORD TO THIS TRANSLATION

Since the day in February 1972 when I introduced Rennes-le-Château and its priest Bérenger Saunière to the world outside France, vast numbers of people have become intrigued... some even obsessed... by the mystery. Innumerable books have been written. Some are the fruit of detailed research — a few are openly fiction — many are just plain dotty. But for those who do not understand the French language, there has always remained a gap. They could not read "the prime source". The first book to tell the strange story — the first book to introduce 'evidence' for the curious happenings at Rennes-le-Château — has never been translated. This book will fill that gap.

The task of translation has not been a simple one. Gérard de Sède writes in a florid — sometimes an opaque — style. To capture his 'spirit' has not been easy. I have, of course, remained scrupulously faithful to his text, which means that I have been obliged to footnote some of his more arcane references. Many of these are well-known to people with a French education and/or for whom they were part of their growing-up. Some of us may know the *Fables of la Fontaine* — but how many of us have heard of du Guesclin? (This, for a French person, is almost like asking: "Have you heard of Wellington?"). De Sède was writing for a French readership — I have done my best to 'build the bridge' for we foreigners...

And then there are his 'errors'... Not all of them are unintentional...! So much that de Sède tells us in this book has been shown to be wrong. So much is obfuscation. So much is simply untrue. And everything is hear-say.

Now — half a life-time after its first appearance — we know so much more. The little local story of the village priest who found a treasure has grown to encompass the whole history of our civilisation. Yet this book still contains mysteries and unanswered questions. In these pages there are things which are passed unnoticed by most readers and yet which merit close attention.

In my book *The Holy Place,* I showed how de Sède's strange caption to the photograph of Station VI of the Stations of the Cross seemed to contain an elaborate hidden message. But what of the other curious captions on that same page? And what of the intriguing — and apparently irrelevant — illustration of the carved door in Rennes-les-Bains? Such things, for most readers, lead to no more than a puzzled shrug of the shoulders and a turning of the page. But these curious obscurities are not accidental. This book was the first important sign-post along a trail of discovery — and it remains key to the mystery. There is much yet to be found. There is much work yet to be done before we can begin to understand the true significance of The *Accursed Treasure*. In your hands, you hold a mysterious, a significant — and a very important — book.

Henry Lincoln,
Rennes-le-Château,
18: iv: 2012

In memory of
Abbé Joseph Courtauly

NOTICE

There is a resemblance between the facts recounted in this book

and an imaginary construct, but this is the result of pure chance.

This is no less strange, for the similarity is striking.

Chapter 1

THE DEVIL IN THE
HOLY WATER STOUP

With Carcassonne behind, the traveller who chooses the beckoning valley of the River Aude soon finds that he has turned his back upon the fertile land. Ahead lie the high, wild valleys, the dense forests, the craggy gorges, a country scoured and tumbled, twisted by the savage claws of nature, scarred and sliced through by the bloody hand of History. This is the Razès — where blue of sky and russet-ochre land clash in a violent confrontation, seeming to play out before our eyes the insoluble discord between Heraclitus and Zenon — between the turbulence of chaos and the fixed, unchanging monotony of order. The holly oaks, the broom, rock roses, lavender and thyme cling with the vigour of despair to the wild crags, torn as by a giant's teeth, pierced through by countless caverns. Here and there, the ruins of a *castel* — unchanging witnesses of times long past, whose story sounds in silence. At Limoux, you must not fail to taste the sparkling Blanquette: go further and it will be too late: the Razès is richer in waters than in wine. Between the vines, nurtured through eight centuries and more, nothing but water seeps from beneath the rocks. This is a country of springs, but also of metals of all kinds. Her waters, mineral rich, are bitter beyond bearing and leave your thirst unquenched; but, bathe in them — as did the queens of old — and you will find they hold the power and the mystery of healing.

The Benedictine abbey of St Hilaire slips past, its cloister curiously adorned with a chess-board carved into the stone. Then, on past the ruins of Alet Cathedral, in ancient days a temple to Diana — raised six centuries ago into a bishopric by Pope John XXII, but fallen now from grace. And then the river's torrent threads the little town of Couiza. Here one turns leftward towards Narbonne, across the first foothills of the Corbières. Then, to the right, a deep-cut roadway flanked by the Peak of Cardou to the left and on the right, three crags, two white, one black as were the Magi: the *Roc de Blanchefort*, the *Roc Pointu* and *Roco Negro*.

This road leads on to Rennes-les-Bains — today, no more than unpretentious thermal spa, but known well to our forbears of a distant past, enjoying a brief moment of brilliance at the time of Rome's conquest. In the village itself, where once an effigy of Isis was unearthed, there are three hot springs: the *Bain de la Reine* (the

Queen's Bath), the *Bain Fort* (the Strong Bath) and the *Bain Doux* (the Gentle Bath). Not too far off are two cold springs — the iron-rich *Source du Cercle* and the one known as *La Madeleine* or *La Gode* in a place called *le Bénitier* (the Holy Water Stoup), where the rivers Blanque and Sals conjoin and where the water bubbles over a slab of greenish rock, decked out with flowerets of crystal.

Most of these springs, which had their birth in the high mountains, appear after long and subterranean journeys, broken by siphons which hold them to a steady flow. In a country where bone-dry summers, following upon the springtime melting of the snows, can cause vast variation in the flowing of the streams; this remarkable regularity — looked on as a miracle of nature — has given birth to hallowed veneration disputed, from one fountain to the next... here by a White Lady, there a Black Virgin. Thus, in Arcadia once, had the River Alph been revered, which of a sudden disappeared, to run '*through caverns measureless to Man*', to surface in far Sicily as Arethusa's sacred Fount.

This mythic parallel appealed to Labouisse-Rochefort, an author of the nineteenth century and tutor to the young Victor Hugo, who began his '*Journey to Rennes-les-Bains*' with the rather limp line:

From thy happy Alpheus, o thou dear Arethusa...

Around this tiny spa the mountain forms a beauteous coronet of russet, white and green where pasture, rock and forest intermix and where still are visible the traces of a vast megalithic enclosure. To the north-west, a *menhir* yet bears the name *Cap de l'Hom* — the Man's Head — as, once, it was adorned with a relief in the likeness of a human face.

Decapitated at the end of the nineteenth century, this strange sculpture can today be found in Rennes-les-Bains, in the garden of the presbytery:[1] some say that it is the face of the Saviour, others, the head of St Dagobert.

To the east, a vast plateau, the *Plateau de Lauzet,* stretches away into the distance. Here is the *Pla de la Coste*, where two boulders, the *Roulers*, each several tons in weight, sway on their bases at the slightest touch. Lower down flows the stream called *l'Hom Mort* — the Dead Man. Further east, the base of a dolmen stands beside the entrance to a mine of jet and a curious mass of rock bears the name *Pierre du Pain* (the Bread Rock), for here a great round stone sits upon a slab, like a loaf of bread upon a table, with five deep impressions, shaped like the imprint of five fingers, which has been dubbed the Devil's Hand. The countryside hereabout has been much enhanced by the Devil... here you will find his Breast, there, his Armchair. And

---

1   Since the devastating flood of 1992, the head has been removed to the safety of the village museum. (Translator's Note)

finally, to the south, towards Serbaïrou, there is a wonderful stone, shaped with geometric perfection in the form of a gaming dice. A phantasmagorical landscape, where it is difficult to distinguish the art of primitive man from the fantasies of nature and which tempts the spirit to pursue an archaeology of the imagination.

"*Here, the divinities of Ancient Gaul bid you welcome, divinities with mute lips of stone. A sombre and sanctified vastness, a pious yet placid terror reigns over these holy places, these sacred sites, which, only with trembling, does one dare approach.*" [2]

Rennes-les-Bains, which was also known as *Règnes*, was once no more than 'The Baths of Rennes' — simply the spa suburb of another Rennes — ancient *Aereda*, which became *Redae* or *Rhedae* and gave its name to *Rhedesium,* the County of Razès. Here, there was once a town of 30,000 inhabitants. With its powerful fortifications, it dominated the plateau which surrounded it. The poet-bishop Théodulf compared its strength to that of Carcassonne in the time of Charlemagne, (*Inde revidentes te, Carcassonna Rhedasque...*) and at the close of the VITH century, the Visigothic kings made it one of their two capitals, the other being Toledo. Its end came in 1361, when it was finally destroyed by the fearsome Aragonese mercenaries of Henri de Trastamare. Today, nothing remains but a lost village with a handful of houses, barely

---

2   Paul Alibert, *Terre de l'Aude.* (Author's Note)

to be found upon the map... Rennes-le-Château.

As the crow flies, the distance between the two Rennes is barely more than three kilometres but, unless you sprout wings, there is a long and winding road to climb before you reach Rennes-le-Château. Filled with hazards, but filled also with the singing of cicadas, fragrant with the scent of the *garrigue*, it is a pathway made for the leisurely wanderer. Set like a chess-piece on the plateau, the village embraces a panorama over the two valleys of the Aude and of the Sals, each one as beautiful as the other. In one direction lie the little towns of Campagne, Laval-Dieu and Le Bezu — three Templar commanderies. In the other, Arques and the ruins of Coustaussa, like the petrified flames of a still-flickering fire which — the name yet bears the echo — was once *custodies*, the vigilant guardian of this wild country.

Rennes-le-Château may, today, seem all but devoid of life, but still she has her *château* and her *châtelain*. With its magnificent Visigothic undercroft — (a rare survival) — its Renaissance façade, its tower... in days past, home to the illustrious families of Hautpoul and Voisin... it is handsome still, if little more now than a ruin. Its sole inhabitant, (one wonders how he manages to survive), will show you — if you can persuade him — the fruits of his strange labours: a collection of stones, in whose weird shapes he has convinced himself that he can see the fossils of men and of animals, born in some far Atlantis to be tossed up here from the ocean deeps. And then there is the atlas, painted by his father who had devoted years of painstaking and gifted brushwork to peopling the whole of France with mythological creatures whose very deeds — (at least according to his cipher system) — have been recorded in the names of even the smallest of our villages. Before the doorway of the *château*, an age-old mulberry spreads its shade; its fruit, like streaming hearts, marking with blood-red stigmata the hands of those who pluck them.[3]

A hundred paces further on, with a terrace which embraces the whole wide horizon, is an assemblage of edifices, uncompromising in their opulence, redolent of late nineteenth century taste and unsightly enough to make one forget their utter incongruity. First there is a two-storied neo-gothic tower, square and crenellated, flanked by a pepper-pot turret and on which one is surprised to read the word "*Magdala*". Then, above a series of rooms, a semi-circular terrace leading to a spacious orangerie, topped by a conical glass roof. These buildings frame a large garden, graced with a water-basin and straight-ruled pathways. Finally — a handsome if frankly bourgeois villa, with a statue of the Sacred Heart above the doorway and with the word "*Bethania*" carved upon its front.

---

3   The mulberry, introduced into France by Pope Clement V (Bertrand de Goth), is known in the Occitanian tongue as *amouré* and in Spanish, *moral*. Beneath this tree, so says the fable, Pyramus and Thisbe died of love. (Author's Note)

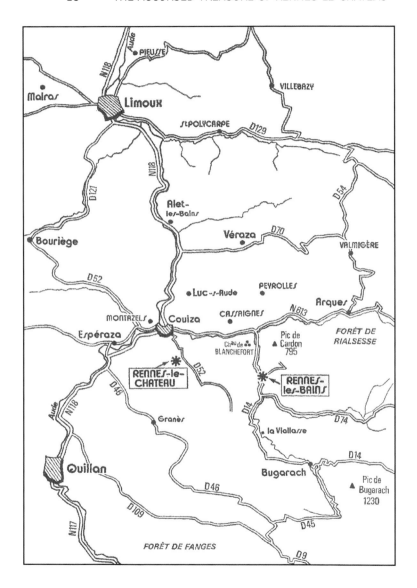

Figure 1.
At the heart of the Razès, the two Rennes:
the upper and the lower.

Near by, the simplicity of the ancient village church, repaired and constantly renewed since the XITH century,[4] makes welcome contrast — at least, when seen from outside. One is barely through the door, however, before sensing an unsettling disquiet. One's first sight is of a deformed devil, weighed down by the Holy Water stoup. Then, little by little, the eye discerns a throng of statues, their faces daubed, clown-like, transfixed in outlandish poses, garish, multi-coloured and holding the visitor with an unnerving and a glassy stare. This is St Sulpice gone mad... a biblical Madame Tussaud's. But soon, despite oneself, one is drawn into this strange world, where every detail seems to be part of the same incomprehensible pattern.

All this was created by someone who still lives on in the memory of those who knew him. We have spoken to each one of them. Piece by piece, the archives have been opened up. Thus have we uncovered the extraordinary story of the Abbé Saunière.

*
* *

François-Bérenger Saunière was a local boy, born in the Aude, at Montazels, on 11TH April 1852. The house where he was born still stands in the village square. Before its door, handsome

---

4   The church was consecrated in 1059 to St Mary Magdalene. (Author's Note)

dolphins, sculpted in the XVIIITH century, spout water into an iron-girdled fountain.[5] Though by no means affluent, his parents were brave enough to raise a family of seven. He was their first-born and — as they say in country parts — you make efforts for your first. Which is doubtless what made it possible for him to enter the church. Ordained in 1879, he is made curate of Alet, then vicar of the humble village of Clat. Perhaps he even allows himself the fleeting dream of a more brilliant career when, after three years, he is promoted to a teaching post at the seminary of Narbonne. But he only lasts there for a month. He is intelligent and wilful, with too much independence of spirit — too strong a personality to suit his superiors. On the 1ST June 1885, they make him priest of Rennes-le-Château. They have no inkling that they have just opened the door to an utterly unprecedented future for the young man whom they have just — apparently so casually — exiled.

At thirty-three... symbolic age for a priest... Bérenger Saunière is to leave behind his mundane life of anonymity. It will not be long before he is reborn as the hero of a fabulous adventure.

Ask the old ladies of his parish, now bent by the weight of years, what they remember of their priest and every one of them will say: "Ah...! He was quite a man!" And in each rheumy

---

5   This fountain was erected in 1751 by Jean-Bernard Carles. (Author's Note)

eye will flash a glint of memory. Photographs show him as big, square-cut, broad shouldered, headstrong. A plebeian countenance, not without a hint of brutishness, accentuated by a heavy jowl but balanced by a broad, high forehead, crowned by a bush of hair. The eyebrows are thick, the dark eyes profound, clear and lively. When, in later life, his gaze becomes disturbingly direct, this is because the man, having lived through one knows not what, has, by his fifties, developed a sort of hard glassiness in his eye. The firm chin, though, is softened by a dimple — in popular imagination, the infallible sign of the seducer.

For such a man, Rennes-le-Château must seem like a prison. The village has no more than a couple of hundred inhabitants. It is poor, and remote. He is priest, it seems, of Nowhere. The only road to it is no more than a rough mule-track. His church, St Mary Magdalene, is all but a ruin. Often, through its crumbling roof, the rain pours down upon him as he speaks the words of the Mass. His presbytery is uninhabitable and for the new curé, there is no alternative but to rent a room from one of his flock, Alexandrine Marro, a rapacious old crone who makes him pay through the nose.

At this time, the clergy are still being paid by the State — but Saunière preaches a rather ill — judged sermon in the run-up to an election. He finds himself labelled a "militant reactionary" and his stipend comes to an abrupt end. Now it is no longer a question of poverty. Now it is hardship — hardship black and unrelieved. No longer able even to pay his rent, there is no alternative for him but to move into a dilapidated shack. We have leafed through his account book for the period: *"Amounts owing to Alexandrine Marro — 1890, July — August: food and bread, 25 francs."* Over a period of sixteen-months, his expenditure is 90 francs; his income: 25 francs... and with wry humour, he adds the note: *"Secret savings: 80 francs 25 centimes."*

Young and fit, he is able to work off his excess energy in hunting and fishing. The smallest of the local streams abound in sleek trout and on the steep slopes of the *garrigue*, he may sometimes even get a shot at that incomparable bird, the *bartavelle*, which some people rather prettily call 'the rare partridge'. And thus, in addition to the sport, there will be the occasional chance to augment his meagre diet.

His hunger for learning is hardly any less. He reads much — and would read more if his purse could allow it. He perfects his Latin, learns some Greek and even attempts Hebrew. He immerses himself in the rich past of the Razès, of the families who had held it and of its once great capital city, into whose remnants an unjust fate has so negligently tossed him. He also spends time with one of his older colleagues, the Abbé Boudet, curé of Rennes-les-Bains, cultured and well read — author of some intriguing works.

And then, of course, there are still the appetites of a young man in his prime. Marie Denarnaud, an eighteen-year-old bonnet-maker, gives up her job at the hat factory to become what one might delicately call his "housekeeper". They say she was jealous and hung sprigs of gorse at the presbytery windows — (the golden flowers were supposed to be a protection against spells). There is nothing in the slightest out of the ordinary in any of this. More unusual, though... as well as more perplexing... is the union which stands the test, the indestructible complicity which, to the very last, will bind together these two so dissimilar individuals. Even in his most ostentatious, his most sybaritic of days, Bérenger will never for an instant dream of parting from Marie. Weighed down by age and loneliness, with well-nigh insupportable problems, Marie is never to betray the secret which she and Bérenger have shared.

If his hardships make him suffer, Saunière grieves even more for the impoverishment of his little church. By good fortune, the Abbé Pons, one of his predecessors, had left six hundred francs to the parish. In 1888, thanks to this little bequest, he is able to carry out the most urgent repairs. Then, by dint of much pleading, he persuades the reluctant municipality to make him the rather more substantial loan of fourteen hundred francs. Towards the end of 1891, with no idea of when or how he is ever going to be able to pay off this debt, he takes the risk of starting the work.

The High Altar is the finest adornment of his church. It rests on two ancient pillars of the Visigothic period, finely carved with crosses and with hieroglyphs. But the stone altar table is in a sorry state, detracting from the beauty of the setting — it has to be replaced. Saunière undertakes the task, with the help of two masons, Rousset and Babou. The heavy slab is removed — and they are surprised to find that one of the pillars is hollow and filled with dried fern. In this nest of leaves they find three wooden tubes, sealed with wax. They open them. Within... parchments.[6]

With witnesses to the discovery, the word soon spreads.

The mayor, with the instinct of the bureaucrat, suggests that the ancient documents should be kept in the village archive. But Saunière thinks differently. Leaving them to gather dust in the *Mairie* will be of no profit to anyone. There are, however, he suggests, collectors of antiques in the big cities who will be prepared to pay a good price for them. It would be better to sell them. He offers to see what he can do.

The curé has cleverly struck the right chord... money is always a welcome guest in

---

6   The Visigothic pillar was found not to be hollow when it was moved into the village museum for safety. It is now suggested that the wooden support for the original pulpit was where Saunière found the parchments. (Translator's note)

the village. The deal is done. Saunière will try to sell the documents, provided he can get back at least the amount which he has borrowed for the work on the church. In this way, there will be nothing to be lost. In addition — (the caution of the peasant is a tenacious weed) — the mayor insists that he must have faithful copies of the documents... for the record. Naturally, the curé is the only person capable of making them. We have had two of these tracings in our hands, to which we shall have cause to refer later.

It is the beginning of 1893 before Saunière makes up his mind to show his bishop what he has found. At this time, the bishop of Carcassonne is the shrewd and intelligent Félix-Arsène Billard, a man with a host of contacts. He makes a very careful examination of what he has been brought: four parchments.

This is the conversation of the two men, as it has been reported to us:

"Are you really thinking of parting with these documents?"

"Frankly, Monseigneur, I haven't the slightest intention. But they're not easy to decipher. I've been working on them every night for more than a year — and I'm getting nowhere. Which is why I've come to you for advice."

"You'll have to go to Paris. I know a few priests with a good knowledge of history and contacts with palaeographers. I'll give you a letter of introduction."

"Paris? But, Monseigneur... I can't afford a trip like that...!"

"Don't worry about it. The diocese will cover your expenses."

"Monseigneur... I've never been outside the Aude. I'm going to be completely out of my depth in Paris..."

"I doubt it, my son. You're not short of 'go' nor of self-confidence. And you'll not want for helping hands there."

"There's another thing, Monseigneur — the mayor's expecting me to sell the documents to repay what I borrowed. As that's out of the question... what do you suggest I tell him when I get back?"

"D'you think the Diocese of Carcassonne's too poor to find fourteen hundred francs? It's no more than a white lie. You can have my absolution in advance."

And so our poverty-stricken country priest leaves for the capital. It's not difficult to imagine him dreaming of himself as a new Rastignac,[7] as he sets out on the train that will carry him to the magic of the City of Light. And it is going to turn out to be quite a trip!

As soon as he arrives, Bérenger Saunière presents his letter of introduction to the Abbé Bieil, the director of St Sulpice, who having examined the four curious documents with some care, asks his visitor to leave them with

---

7   A provincial social climber who figures in novels by Balzac. (Translator's note)

him for a week in order to have them looked at by specialists.

What can one do in Paris with pockets virtually empty? Saunière has no idea; but fortunately, Bieil introduces him to his nephew, Ané, a publisher of religious books, who offers to put him up. He also introduces him to his great-nephew, Emile Hoffet. This young cleric has barely started his career but, at twenty, he already speaks several languages. He is interested in the Middle Ages and is studying palaeography and cryptography. Ahead of him lies a long career of research which is to take him to the Vatican on more than one occasion and lead him into studies of the occult and secret societies.

His new-found friends help the country priest to realise how undeserved is the reputation for dreariness of the church built by Olier, the visionary Abbé of Pibrac. In fact, nothing can be less banal than the church of Saint-Sulpice, this "new Temple of Solomon". Saunière must have been surprised to see the Stations of the Cross placed in reverse order, the astronomical gnomon, the inscriptions — now, alas, hacked out — which marked the Paris Meridian and the three handsome Holy Water Stoups; he must have admired the Delacroix paintings and Signol's extraordinary Crucifixion; he must have read the plaque which commemorates the visit of Pope Pius VII in 1804, on the feast day of Saint-Dagobert, which the pontiff followed by a trip to the Razès.

Bérenger also spent some time at the Louvre museum; and after reading up on their creators, he purchased copies of three paintings which, on his return, he will hang on the walls of his humble dwelling: *The Shepherds of Arcadia,* by Poussin; *Saint-Antony Hermit*, by David Teniers and a portrait of Pope Celestin V which he found, who-knows-where? A singularly curious collection.

And it was not just painting which Saunière discovered in Paris, there was also music. Certainly, Erato [8] presented herself in a guise which was not lacking in charm. This period, too, had its Callas: her name was Emma Calvé, a great beauty who had made her debut in Brussels nine years earlier in Gounod's *Faust.* The twenty-four year-old 'Marguerite' was an immediate sensation, with her extraordinary soprano voice and her gifted acting. She had just come back from London, hailed as the greatest opera singer of the age. Queen Victoria, having heard her in *Carmen*, had invited her to Windsor and had commissioned a portrait bust of her. For the moment she was between two triumphant tours and back in Paris, where Massenet was writing *Sappho* for her. How, barely arrived in the capital, the poor parish priest of Rennes-le-Château was able to make the acquaintance

---

8   Erato is, in fact, the Muse of love poetry. The Muse of Music is Euterpe. Perhaps the author had 'erotic' in mind? (Translator's note)

of this diva, we cannot easily explain.[9] The fact remains, however, that he did... and well enough for the prima-donna to waste no time in proving to him that, off-stage, she had little in common with the Poetess of Lesbos. Their liaison, in no way concealed, was to continue for a number of years. Bérenger, however, did not forget the purpose of his journey. On the appointed day, he is back knocking on the Abbé Bieil's door. We have not been able to establish with certainty what was said, or what passed between the two men on this occasion. It seems, in fact, that the documents were not returned to Saunière or at least, not all of them. In any event, the end result must have been unclear, as Monseigneur Billard thought it well, in March 1901, to undertake a trip to Saint-Sulpice to clarify matters.

Had there been some sort of deal in which the curé handed over the precious documents in exchange for equally precious information? If such were the case, the outcome is to show that the price he paid must have seemed trifling to our 'pilgrim'.

*
* *

After his stay of three hectic weeks, Bérenger Saunière returns home. In Carcassonne

9   It was, perhaps, Hoffet who introduced Saunière to Emma Calvé. Hoffet and the singer were both friends of the composer Claude Debussy, at whose home Emma and Bérenger may have met. (Author's note)

he makes a more-or-less accurate report to his bishop, who hands him two thousand francs. This is a little more than he needs to pay off the mayor, who is told that the documents have been sold.

No sooner returned, our curé gets back to work with the help of several youngsters, one of whom, Antoine Verdier, who was still alive in 1962, we were able to interview. The first thing he does is to lift a particular flag-stone which lies at the foot of the altar. The face turned to the earth is then seen to be carved. Now known as the "*Dalle du Chevalier*" (the Knight's Stone), this very ancient object — Merovingian or Carolingian — was kept for a decade in Carcassonne Museum and is now, at the request of the mayor and villagers, returned to its original home. It consists of two panels. The one on the left, extremely worn, could represent a knight sounding a horn while his horse is drinking. On the right, as far as one can now tell, is the representation of either two riders on the same horse, or a knight holding in one hand a sceptre and with the other, supporting a child on the animal's neck.[10]

At the place which has been uncovered, Saunière orders a hole to be dug to a depth of about a metre and then, using lunch-time

---

10   Stylistically, this stone seems to resemble depictions of the Celtic horse goddess Epona. It can certainly have nothing to do with the "two knights on one horse" image of the Knights Templar, which seems to be the implication here. (Translator's note)

as an excuse, he sends his helpers away and remains in the church alone. At the bottom of the excavation, however, the workmen have had time to uncover two skeletons [11] and to catch a glimpse of a pot filled with shiny objects which Saunière claims are worthless metal tokens. From these first-hand statements, we can only be sure that the curé now digs here and there in the church and finds more objects, doubtless very old, but of which it is no longer possible to be certain as to their origin, nature or value.

But it is also at this time that the Abbé Saunière undertakes a singular task of his own. Each day, accompanied by the faithful Marie (who is irreverently labelled his Madonna), he leaves the village carrying a basket on his back. The couple spend long hours wandering the plateau for miles around. From far off, one can sometimes see Bérenger bend to pick up a stone and put it into his basket or perhaps toss it away. In the evening, he returns, bowed under the weight, to explain cheerfully to anyone intrigued by his doings:

"It's to prettify the little garden beside our cemetery. I intend to build a grotto which will be rather attractive; so I'm going to need a lot of carefully chosen stones of the right shape and colour. Marie's helping me find them and we'll spend as much time as it takes."

---

11   Re-opened a few years ago, this grave contained a most curious skull, which I shall deal with later. (Author's Note)

Nobody argued with this explanation, as Saunière did indeed build the grotto, stone by stone, with his own hands. This baroque monument still stands, though not as it once was: it has been partly destroyed by someone unknown, which is a great pity for the curious visitor.[12]

Bérenger found it somewhat more difficult, though, to explain why he spent his nights shut in the cemetery. There, up against the church, were two tombstones which marked the grave of Marie de Négri d'Ables, wife of François d'Hautpoul, Marquis de Blanchefort, Seigneur of Rennes. She died a few years before the French Revolution of 1789 and the curé Antoine Bigou, her chaplain and confessor, had lovingly composed her epitaph.

But if Bérenger Saunière loved stones to the point of carrying them on his back by the basket- load, it seems that in one way or another, he objected to these two tombstones. For not only did he undertake to carry them from one end of the cemetery to the other, but more — with stone-cutter's tools, he patiently polished away the inscriptions on one of them and a little later, caused the other one to 'disappear'.

This time there were objections to his actions: in the eyes of even the most ardent unbeliever, graves are sacred. Moreover, in the cemetery, the curé is no longer 'at home'. In

_____

12   Now rebuilt. Early photographs show that the original may have been slightly lower. (Translator's note)

1895, the villagers lodged a formal complaint and Saunière was instructed by the municipality henceforth to leave the dead to sleep in peace.

Some time later Ernest Cros, an engineer, a keen amateur archaeologist who had moved into the area, enquired of Saunière:

"M. le curé, why, did you move that tomb?"

"Well, every year several of my flock die; the cemetery is now too small to provide decent graves for them. So I've made this ossuary for the most ancient remains. I had to find a cover for it and so I've used this tombstone."

"But how can a cultivated man like you, who loves the past, efface an ancient inscription?"

"It wouldn't make much sense on an ossuary," Bérenger replied, evasively, quickly changing the subject.

What Saunière didn't know was that his labour — or his precaution — had been in vain. In fact, before he obliterated them, the rather intriguing inscriptions on the tomb of the Marquise de Blanchefort had been copied by visiting local archaeologists. One of them had thus been reproduced in the *Bulletin of the Society of Scientific Research of the Aude*; the other figures in Eugène Stublein's *Carved Stones of the Languedoc*, a work which is today of extreme rarity.

The first was, on a vertical headstone:

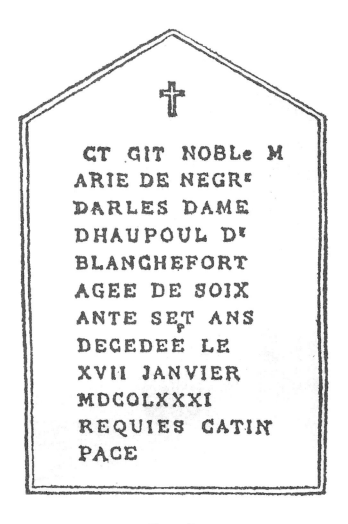

Figure 2.

The second, a rectangular stone, lay at the foot of the other and is now in the cemetery of Rennes-le-Château.[13] It bore the following inscription:

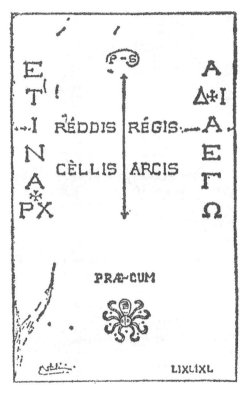

Figure 3.
(Copy by Eugène Stublein, provided by M.R. Chésa).

---

13   Unfortunately, this is no longer the case. Shattered into pieces by treasure-hunting vandals, the few remaining fragments now lie in the garden beside the Villa Bethania. (Translator's Note)

Once he has finished building his grotto, Bérenger Saunière takes to travelling. Laden with a suitcase, so heavy that he sometimes carries it on his shoulder like a Cross, sometimes even on a donkey, he scrambles often down the tortuous track which leads from the village to the outside world. Where is he going? Nobody knows. What is he up to? One can only wonder. Sometimes he is away for five or six days, sometimes even longer. He calls often at Montazels, his home village, where lives one of his brothers — also a priest — but his visits there are brief. And indeed, at this time, he sends letters to various people, posted from border-towns: Perpignan, Nice, Lons-le-Saunier, Valenciennes... We also have his correspondence with a bank in Paris; the Petitjean Bank in the rue Montmartre; both sides dealing with various transactions in somewhat obscure phrases. This bank even sent an emissary to Rennes-le-Château — a M. de Beauvière. We also know that he had dealings with a jeweller in Mazamet.

In any event, our man keeps his travels secret. Before each trip, he prepares a number of typed letters... one can appreciate the humour:

Rennes-le-Château,.........

M......

With the most humble respect, I have read the letter which you have done me the honour to send and to which I am paying the greatest attention. Please accept that I am quite aware of the significance of the question you have raised, but it requires due consideration. I therefore beg you to allow a few days for my response, as I am presently dealing with a matter of some urgency.

Yours etc ...

B. Saunière (Rev)

These all-purpose letters are generally addressed to the bishop, the vicar general or to local priests. If one of them should unexpectedly try to get in touch, the faithful Marie Denarnaud needs only to add the date: the postmark will prove that our curé — (who has gone who-knows-where) — has not left the area. And so the game is played.

At the same time, postal orders in Marie's name begin to flood in from Germany, Spain, Switzerland, Italy, sometimes coming from religious communities and adding up to perhaps as much as 110 to 150 francs per day.

And this is when Bérenger Saunière, penniless so little time before, starts to spend — and to spend wildly and extravagantly. First in 1896, he begins, at his own expense, to repair his church. And now it is no longer a case of minor repairs; he restores the entire edifice from top to bottom. A team of workers, following his detailed instructions, move or enlarge windows. They build a room against the sacristy with access through a secret door hidden in a cupboard. They cut a hole in a wall to create a staircase leading to the pulpit. Occasionally, the workers are baffled by their instructions: why, for example, at the end of the nave near the entrance, does he make them place sixty four square tiles, alternately black and white? But Saunière is authoritarian and personally supervises every tiny detail. Argument is futile: in any case, what would be the point, as he always pays on the nail?

Our priest then brings in a team of sculptors and painters from Toulouse, Bordeaux and elsewhere, with the task of decorating the church, both inside and out — providing them with bed and board, as always out of his own pocket. These artists will stay for several months, creating the decoration of the arch above the entrance, the statues, the paintings, the stained-glass windows, the Stations of the Cross, the pulpit. And yet again, Saunière, a patron endowed with atrocious, if fastidious taste, is both inspiration and director. He composes the inscriptions himself; he even goes so far as to have the Calvaire re-made three times, because he is not satisfied with the inclination of Christ's head! This Calvaire alone cost 11,000 francs. From time to time, Bérenger himself wields palette and paintbrush: the painted Magdalen beneath the altar is his work.

By 1897, all is ready and Bérenger wastes no time before inviting his bishop to inaugurate it. Logically, Mgr Billard should have been utterly delighted with his subordinate's work. After all, without asking his superiors for a penny, he has in no time restored the ruined buildings — which should have been the responsibility of the Church. However, as soon as he arrives, the prelate is gripped by an indefinable discomfort... as you will be, when you visit this strange place of worship. Even though he was used to the hideous imagery of the period, it may have crossed his mind, as it did that of Léon Bloy, [14] that ugliness is itself blasphemous. Or perhaps the bishop could not escape from the spell cast by the strange world of Bérenger's imaginings? He seems maliciously to be playing with words when he has Jacob's awe-struck cry at Bethel carved above the entrance: *Terribilis est locus iste*. Yes, this place is indeed terrible! Perhaps finally, on reading another of the inscriptions: *Mea domus orationis vocabitur*, (*My house is called the house of prayer*), [15] the prelate remembered the continuation of this gospel verse: "*but you have made it a den of thieves*"... he can hardly have avoided the allusion. In any event, he finds the spectacle hard to stomach. He hastens from the church, hurriedly blesses the Calvaire, mumbles a few polite words and leaves. Henceforth, Rennes-le-Château will be excluded from his list of pastoral visits.

But Saunière's thirst for building is still far

---

14   Léon Bloy (1846-1917) — French Catholic writer. (Translator's Note)

15   In fact, Saunière has written (correctly): *Domus mea domus orationis vocabitur*, 'My house shall be called the house of prayer'. (Translator's Note)

from quenched. In 1900, he buys a large amount of land stretching to the very edge of the rocky, red and white escarpment on which the village is perched.The site is superb, the panorama stretching as far as the eye can see. There, above the abyss, he has a crenellated tower erected, two storeys high, which he will call *Magdala*. The lower room will be his bedroom and here no-one may call upon him — though some may be invited. The room above will be his library. As always, the builder will be no more than an obedient servant — Saunière is effectively the architect; and even though stone is available locally, his comes from a considerable distance on the backs of mules, without consideration of cost or difficulty of transport. With the precision of a mathematician, he keeps a watchful eye upon the orientation of his tower. Then he lays out the curving, crenellated belvedere, along which one may stroll to enjoy the landscape in all its aspects. At the other end of his domain he builds the spacious villa which he will name *Bethania.* Then he builds the orangerie and lays out the park with its paths and water features, fed by three immense storage tanks. Some archaeologists who pay a visit are amazed:

"M. L'Abbé Saunière makes us welcome and takes pleasure in showing us round his beautiful establishment which seems without question to be a lost oasis in the midst of a desert [...] the plateau is taken up by a kitchen garden where the vegetables he is growing would make a market gardener green with envy; then there

is an orchard and a handsome leisure garden, shaded by a terrace where one can delight in a magnificent panorama. To the south there is a tower which seems to watch over this charming spot: and here we were able to enjoy a few restful moments while admiring the rich library it contains." [16]

And this domain could indeed hold its head high... it had cost a million francs.

Even more astonishing is the life which, henceforth, Bérenger will live in this setting. For him, Magdala is to become doubly his ivory tower. Here, far from the vain worries of the world, he will doubtless sometimes fall to thinking: "Let the ignorant return to his science and the fisherman to his nets." Bethania, on the other hand, will become his royal court, the House of God, open to all, where guests will find crisp sheets and a groaning board. Malicious tongues are soon sneering, "It's a bit like the work-house".

In fact Bérenger Saunière, as if he has a bottomless purse, gives free rein to every caprice of his fantastical imagination. Not satisfied with providing himself with the library of which he has always dreamed, he brings in a bookbinder from Toulouse, to whom he gives bed and board for months on end, as well as a photographer to capture all the wonders of the countryside. He makes a collection of

16   A. Fages, *Bulletin de la Société des Etudes scientifiques de l'Aude,* vol XX, 1909. (Author's note)

ten thousand picture postcards, another of a hundred thousand postage stamps. He collects antique furniture, fabrics, porcelain. His two dogs, Faust and Pomponnet, are not company enough: he creates a zoo which he fills with fish, peacocks, monkeys and parrots. His barnyard ducks are spoon-fed with biscuits. Even though he lives in the land of the cassoulet, he orders his beans from Lille! His follies, as childish as they are costly, still amaze those who knew him in his spendthrift days.

The Villa Bethania is never empty. Priests such as the Lazarist Ferrafiat rub shoulders with local bigwigs; guests come from Paris, such as the Arts Minister Dujardin-Baumetz, beautiful women, grand ladies: Emma Calvé, of course, but also the writer Andrée Bruguière who liked to call herself the Viscountess d'Artois, as well as the very authentic Marquise du Bourg de Bozas. The most mysterious guest is the one the villagers can only call "The Foreigner". The incognito is hiding the Archduke Jean de Habsbourg, cousin of the Emperor of Austria-Hungary.

Everything is organised to provide this motley assemblage with an enchanted stay: a white-apronned and frilly-bonneted maid is on hand to serve Marsala, Malvoisie and Tokai. The drink flows freely, as Saunière's account books testify: "1ST November 1900: 1 cask of Martinique rum, caisse ABC No 1031: 45 litres at 2 francs = 90 francs. 50 litres of rum at 2.35 francs = 117.5 francs (superb rum, well-nigh historic), 33 litres of Haut Barsac white wine, 33 litres Malvoisie, 17 litres Gold Quinquina, 53 litres Banyuls, 12 litres Muscat."

Has Marie given up on jealousy? She seems to have resigned herself, without too much trouble, to seeing the flock of petticoats twirling about Bérenger. Perhaps it's just her peasant philosophy, or perhaps she's simply gratified by the rapid ascent of the man whose poverty she has shared. This 'High Society' may well consider her naïve: but she well knows how irreplaceable she is. No-one knows Saunière as she knows him; no-one has, nor ever will, make the 'fantastic journey' with him...

To be fair, it must be said that our luxury-loving curé also devotes himself just as much to good works, even if some of the delights which he provides for his flock can seem somewhat bizarre. The famous Visigothic pillar from the altar, he now has moved to the church garden, though not without having part of it polished in order to engrave the inscription: "MISSION 1891". Above it, he has set a rather unpretty confection: the Virgin of Lourdes giving to the faithful a piece of advice which well demonstrates Bérenger's sense of humour: "PENITENCE! PENITENCE!" The villagers would have found the joke in somewhat dubious taste as, in the Aude at the time, the life of the peasant was a frugal one. This, however, seems to matter little, as the curé was making an annual donation of five thousand francs to the village funds, besides making gifts of ten to fifteen thousand francs to the poorest families: veritable small fortunes. The inaugural ceremony for the monument was a memorable occasion; a huge firework display accompanied the unveiling of the statue: Saunière surrounded the area with a fuse linking hundreds of fire-crackers whose salvos could be heard for miles around!

So one must make allowances for the curé. Besides, if one can be hard on the priest when he is being a Holy Monster, one can, in this anti-clerical Midi, turn a blind eye to his human frailties. And this is only apparently paradoxical. At Rennes-le-Château the Abbé Saunière is remembered above all as a rather unconventional "gay dog" — "one of the lads". Certainly he set tongues wagging and got the imaginations working. In these backwoods where distractions are rare — his life, his caprices, his follies, his baroque ideas, reflect more than a touch of the unusual. Every day was a free circus, for which he had created the décor and in which he was impresario, director and star, rolled into one. Most of all, he was loved because he was a true 'local boy', a native of the Land of Oc, where no virtue is more highly esteemed than wholehearted conviviality and stylish liberality... even when there is a touch of ostentation.

What is more surprising is that the ecclesiastical authorities seem to be not the slightest bit concerned by the strange behaviour of the Abbé Saunière. Just as they have kept their eyes closed to his liaison with an eighteen-year-old servant-girl, they choose to pay no attention to the wild goings-on at the villa Bethania and don't even enquire about the source of the funds which are enabling the curé to enjoy such a lavish life-style. True, this is a time when bishops have worries enough of their own: the Law on Congregations [17] has just been passed, the Law of Separation [18] is on its way. Relations with the State are growing ever more strained. And perhaps Mgr Billard also has his own good reasons for being cautious in his treatment of this *enfant terrible*.

But, in 1902, Mgr de Beauséjour succeeds Mgr Billard to the See of Carcassonne and in the following year, Pius X succeeds Leo XIII on the papal throne. At a stroke, everything changes for Bérenger Saunière.

The new Bishop proceeds cautiously, a step at a time. First, he instructs Bérenger to take a retreat in a monastery for a week or so. But it's going to take more than this to curb a spirit of this kind. In January 1908, he offers him the parish of Coustauge: the Carthusian monastery of Durban is not far off and one may think that this very proximity is enough to worry

---

17   The *loi sur les congrégations*, controlling religious institutions, had been passed on 1ST July 1901. (Translator's note)
18   The *loi de séparation*, which finally separated Church and State, was passed on 9TH December 1905. (Translator's note)

our man! [19] But Saunière, in his best hand, sends his bishop a rather insolent response: "I cannot leave a parish where my interests retain me."

Indeed? What 'interests'? Mgr de Beauséjour decides to find out more and summons the curé to Carcassonne. But — alas! Bérenger is unwell. For every summons, there is another illness. Each time, the letter of apology is accompanied by a medical certificate. Certificates of pure convenience, provided by Dr Rocher of Couiza who baldly writes to Saunière: My dear friend, I forward the certificate which you have asked for. If it won't do, tell me what you want and I'll be delighted to send something more satisfactory.

If his diplomatic illnesses prevent Bérenger from going to Carcassonne, they do not hinder his jaunts abroad under cover of the ingenious postal system which he has created with Marie's help.

But after a year of this little game, Saunière can no longer avoid a visit to the bishop's palace.

"Your life-style seems to be somewhat grander than my own", Mgr de Beauséjour tells him, "and I wish you to give me an account of the source of your wealth which seems to be as

---

19   This sentence is curious! There seems, superficially, to be a mis-spelling of the name of this village, which is, in fact, Coustouge — (correct in the MS.). But Durban is nowhere near — it is not even in the same Département!) (Translator's note)

much out-of-the-blue as it is substantial".

"Alas, Monseigneur, you are asking of me the one thing which I cannot reveal. Considerable sums of money have been given to me by souls whose sins have been great and to whom, by God's grace, I have been able to show the way of penitence. You well know that I may not, by giving you their names, betray the secrets of the confessional."

The bishop could have replied that his visitor was showing some gall in exhorting others to repentance. But the curé's argument was both astute and undeniable: anyone making a gift can, indeed, insist on remaining anonymous.

"Very well, I'm prepared to acknowledge your scruples; but if you can't reveal the source of your income, you can at least explain what you're doing with it."

"I'm not obliged to account to you, Monseigneur. The donors have given me a free hand in the use of their money, as it was given to me personally and not to the Church. As they continue with their generosity, isn't this proof that I have not abused their trust? Beyond that... what have you to reproach me with? When I arrived, my parish was in a parlous state. I have rebuilt and embellished the church without asking you for a penny... I deserve congratulation rather than suspicion. After all", Saunière continues brazenly, "isn't it supposed to be for my superiors to provide Rennes-le-Château with a church that's fit for its flock, as well as a decent lodging for its priest?"

"This doesn't alter the fact that the opulence of your 'Domaine' can create scandal..."

"If I have considered nothing to be too beautiful, Monseigneur," the curé complacently replies, "it's because, when I die, the place will become a retirement home for aged priests."

But the bishop is not prepared to give up: a little later, he orders Saunière to send him an exact written account of his expenditure. We have, in our hands, the laborious rough-draft of the note sent by the curé. With a good deal of fiddling, he has managed to reduce his spending to one hundred and ninety-three thousand francs. This sum, not a small one by any means — (as a comparison, it's worth remembering that, at the time, the annual income of an ambassador was forty thousand francs) — did not amount to even a fifth of Bérenger's actual outlay. For example, he gives ten thousand francs as the total cost of all his furnishings, when his solid oak library alone was worth at least that amount! It goes without saying that there were no receipts to accompany the note; and the curé — who kept a record of his smallest outgoings to the last penny — claimed that he didn't keep accounts.

Tired of the defiance, Mgr de Beauséjour changes tactics.

"These funds, for which you can provide no explanation," he tells Saunière, "must be coming from trafficking in masses."

Our hero had little trouble in dealing with this. At the time, a mass cost half a franc; without permission, a priest had the right to celebrate no more than three masses per day. One hundred and ninety-three thousand francs add up to three hundred and eighty-six thousand masses! In order to say them, Saunière would have to live for another three hundred and fifty years! Furthermore, each one of his parishioners would have had to have ordered more than three thousand masses!

Be that as it may: the bishop has decided to break the obdurate curé. Sticking to his accusation of simony, he lays it before the Diocesan Ecclesiastical Court. Saunière does not appear before the Court and drags the matter out for six months. On the 5TH December 1910, he is found guilty by default and declared *suspens a divinis* which, in simple terms, means that he no longer has the right to say mass, nor to administer the sacraments.

But far from giving way, in 1911, the curé of Rennes-le-Château lodges an appeal with Rome. His lawyer, Canon Huguet of the diocese of Agen, spends two years at his expense, at the Vatican, demonstrating the illogicality and unrealistic nature of the accusation of trafficking in masses. In 1913, Mgr de Beauséjour's case is dismissed: Bérenger has won.[20]

His success, however, was short-lived. From some unknown source, an important Vatican personage seems to have been informed that this apparently minor local quarrel was concealing a horse of an altogether different colour. Rome encouraged the bishop of Carcassonne to lodge a counter-appeal. On the 11TH April 1915, without any new charges being brought against him, the curé of Rennes-le-Château is definitively interdicted. He is ordered to hand over the presbytery and the church to his successor, the Abbé Henri Marty.

But this is a clear case of not understanding Bérenger Saunière. In 1905, the law separating Church and State had been passed. Churches and presbyteries had become the property of the local commune. Almost immediately, Bérenger — (formerly considered a reactionary, but who is now mixing with the radicals) — leased the presbytery from the municipality: in the name of Marie. So the new curé is reduced to living miles away, down in the valley. And on Sundays when, perspiring and out of breath, he climbs up to the village, he finds himself gazing at empty pews. The real Mass, with a packed congregation, is no more than a few steps away. It is the one that Saunière is celebrating in the

---

20   At the Bishopric in Carcassonne, there are those who sometimes deny that Saunière's case went as far as Rome, nevertheless some of the documents pertaining to the hearing in Rome are to be found in the private archive of a collector, M. Noël Corbu. (Author's note)

chapel which he has just built on to his villa.

These disputes with the hierarchy, which deprive him of his convenient obscurity — and then the War, which has closed the frontiers, are all upsets to Saunière's activities. No more journeys — so no more money. In 1911, he asks for a loan from the Crédit Foncier Bank and is thinking about selling some of his property. In 1915, the cabinet-maker who has made-to-measure all his furniture, is chasing him for a large unpaid bill. To add to the blow delivered by the Church, some kindly souls, as is always the case, are looking for a chance to administer the *coup de grace*. This is a time when espionage is in the air: "Careless talk costs lives", "Watch what you say... the enemy is listening!" Saunière's somewhat unusual way of life naturally lays him open to suspicion. There are some who whisper that he is a German spy; that his Villa is being used by the Kaiser's Secret Service. Some even go so far as to claim that he has a cannon hidden in his tower!

But it's obvious that this 'devil of a fellow' is not going to take long to find a way out of his money worries. In fact, he is soon coming up with new schemes, more imaginative, more extravagant than ever. As he would like to own a car, but there is no drivable route, he dreams up the idea of having a four-kilometre-long road constructed to link Rennes-le-Château to Couiza. He decides to lay on running water for all the inhabitants of the village and to rebuild the ancient city walls. He thinks of building a new chapel in the middle of the cemetery, with a baptismal pool, as in the days of the first Christians. But his visions grow even more grand: he orders the building of a seventy-metre-high tower whose interior walls, from top to bottom, will be lined with books. This Tower of Babel library, worthy of the imagination of a Borgia, will have a spiral staircase and from its summit, like a muezzin, the Abbé will preach to his flock of the new religious ideas which are beginning to germinate in his brain...

Simply the dreams of a megalomaniac? Not in the slightest. Not only does he have the plans for these astonishing works drawn up by the architect Caminade, — (stolen by one-knows-not-whom, these plans disappeared in 1930) — but, on 5TH January 1917, [21] he signs the estimate for the work to be carried out by the builder Elie Bot... it will amount to 8 million gold francs!

Bérenger Saunière did not have the time to realise these grandiose projects. Two days later, on 17TH January, he had a stroke in the doorway of the Tour Magdala. Dr Courrent, a doctor from Carcassonne, [22] who was also an archaeologist, came to his bedside. The patient still had some strength, but he had been burning

---

21   This date would seem to be a typographical error (see para. following). I note, however, that the error is repeated in all the contemporary editions... as well as in the Manuscript. (Translator's note)

22   Dr Courrent's practice was much closer — in Rennes-les-Bains, in fact. (Translator's note)

the candle at both ends. Perhaps he was past cure...

Bérenger Saunière gave up the ghost on 22ND January 1917 at the age of sixty — five years. His body was exposed on the belvedere, draped in a covering which was adorned with red tassels. The whole village filed past in final homage, each person taking, in souvenir, one of the tassels. Now he rests in the cemetery where he passed so many nights in erasing an epitaph.[23] No longer does anyone come to lay flowers on his grave... now fierce-thorned brambles are its covering.

When he felt his end approaching, Bérenger sent for the Abbé Rivière, priest of the nearby village of Esperaza — a man who enjoyed the good life and who had been his long-time friend, remaining steadfast even when he had been suspended. Open minded, he knew that the flesh is weak and believed that God would show compassion toward his prodigal children. What transpired between these two priests? We shall never know. But, when Rivière left his dying friend, he was white and shaken. Nor did he quickly recover. He became withdrawn, taciturn, silent. For the rest of his life, he was never seen to smile. What terrible secret had been confided to him? Or what spiritual abyss had he seen opening before his eyes? Did the soul

---

23   This, tragically, is no longer true. His body now lies outside the cemetery, in unconsecrated ground, where it was removed in 2004, on the instructions of the village mayor. (Translator's note)

of Bérenger seem to him already transformed into one of those rocks against which even the mercy of God shatters its wings? Did he think that he was leaving his friend at the Gates of Hell? Whatever happened, something unheard of followed. It was not until two days after his death that the curé of Rennes-le-Château received from him the last rites. To the very end and even beyond, Bérenger Saunière would keep his aura of mystery.

Even so, he does not seem to have been fashioned of that stuff from which great sinners are made. At the time of the Second Empire, what could a poor family with many children do with a bright lad, except make him a priest? The tragedy is that Bérenger was born to be an adventurer, an explorer, an entrepreneur, a buccaneer or a soldier: anything but a priest. When his superiors realised this, did they truly think that they could change him by exiling him to a forgotten mountain-top? These men, whose vocation makes them so careful — had they really looked at him? Could they not see the energy and limitless appetite expressed in his face, or guess that here was something of the soldier of fortune, the blood of the Aragou, the fearsome Aragonese mercenary? To Rennes-le-Château he brings all the pent-up desires of a child of poverty — from the desperately coveted playthings to the books beyond his means, not to mention the village fetes where his seminarist's robe prevents him from matching himself against the other lads at the shooting galleries, the drinking and the wenching. And as he grows in years and in understanding, his desires only increase and grow more complicated. Who, then, can condemn Bérenger Saunière simply for his profligate, hot-headed nature? What Mephistopheles, disguised as Faust or Pomponnet, could have stolen from him all that remained of his youthful nature? The end of the XIXTH century now seems so dull to us, that we sometimes forget how much it was secretly haunted by the Devil. Bloy and Huysmans bear witness to this obsession — as does Barrès. Have you, in fact, read *La Colline inspirée*? [24]

After the death of Bérenger Saunière, his books, his pictures, a good part of his papers and even some of the stones with which he had adorned his domaine disappear as if by magic. [25]

When, with an impatience which can be imagined, the will was opened of this man who had thrown millions out of the window, his heirs — and the bishopric — were dumbfounded. The curé owned nothing... had never owned anything. All his goods and chattels — everything — belonged to his housekeeper, Marie Denarnaud.

24   Léon Bloy (1846-1917), Joris-Karl Huysmans (1848-1907) and Maurice Barrès (1862-1923) are novelists. Barrès's novel *La Colline inspirée* ('The Mystic Mountain') would seem to be the "imaginary concept" to which de Sède makes reference in his 'Notice' at the beginning of this book. (Translator's note)
25   Part of his library seems to have been dispersed by Gacon, a book-dealer from Lyon. The second Visigothic pillar from the church was apparently taken to the château at Cabrières, near Millau, by Emma Calvé. (Author's note)

Bethania was closed. Those who had once been invited there were now quick to forget the place. Did not the Christ of the Sacred Heart who towers over the façade open his arms as much to bid farewell to those who departed as to greet those who entered?

The doorway opened as wide in one direction as it did in the other.

Chapter 2

THE GOLD OF RENNES

In following us in our account of Bérenger Saunière's wild spending spree, the reader cannot have failed to attempt to calculate the present valuation of the amount which he spent — or claimed to have spent. [26]

If one accepts the amount given in the 'fiddled' accounts which he sent to his bishop, Bérenger admitted to having spent, on the building works and the first repairs of the church alone, four hundred and twenty five thousand francs. As one commentator has remarked, "*it*

---

26   The first paragraphs of this chapter deal, with some complexity, with the complications of converting '*francs-or'* — gold francs or '*Napoleons'* — into '*francs lourds'* (the currency of 1967) and '*anciens francs'* (old francs). I have given an abbreviated translation, as the details are meaningless to those not conversant with the obsolete currencies of France. For readers who are interested in the precise numbers given by de Sède, the complete original text, with translation, is appended as an End Note. (Translator's note)

was certainly a considerable sum for the time". [27] But we know without question, from invoices, that these works in fact cost one million and thirty thousand francs.

To this must be added the whole of the decoration of the church. In this case, most of the bills are missing. But as the Calvaire alone came to twenty-four thousand, two hundred francs (11,000 gold francs), one may estimate without too much risk of error, that this prodigiously expensive decoration must have cost about five hundred thousand francs.

One must also take into consideration the sumptuous life-style of our man, keeping 'open house', as he did, for more than ten years, between the year of his discovery and his first money problems. To keep this up, three thousand francs per month would seem a perfectly reasonable estimate which, in ten years, amounts to three hundred and sixty thousand francs.

But we also have very good reason to believe that the curé of Rennes-le-Château passed over to Mgr Billard the sum of one million gold francs [28] which the bishop used for the restoration of the Dominican monastery of Prouilles. Lastly, one must think that Bérenger would not, just before his death, have signed a

---

27   René Descadeillas: *Notice sur Rennes-le-Château et l'abbé Saunière.* (Author's note)
28   The author equates one 'gold franc' to 2.20 francs of 1967. (Translator's note)

contract for eight million gold francs if he did not have the means to settle it.

Thus, between 1891 and 1917, our hero would have got through, in total, an amount of something between a minimum of fifteen million and a maximum of twenty four million gold francs!

In any case, it matters little whether the sum was fifteen or twenty four millions; such amounts lead inevitably to the question — whence came the sudden wealth of the impoverished Abbé Saunière?

These figures immediately demolish the accusation of trafficking in masses made by Mgr de Beauséjour. What point was there in claiming that Saunière was gathering his clients throughout France by means of 'small ads', since he could not produce a single press cutting to support the allegation? And he did, by the way, later admit to one of his friends, Mgr de Cabrières: "I needed a pretext, but I never believed it". The accusation was weak enough, as we have seen, for Rome to reject it: neither is there any reason for us to do otherwise.

It has also been claimed that the curé's fortune came from the generosity of Emma Calvé. This explanation is no more reasonable than the other: in fact, even though it was much talked about, Bérenger's liaison with the diva was no more than a passing one. One meeting in Paris and a few visits by Emma to Rennes-le-Château... and that is all. At the time when

Bérenger is living his high-life, Emma Calvé is away in the United States for four years. And in 1914 she puts an end to the liaison by marrying the tenor Gasbarri: one can hardly expect that, three years later, she will be promising to finance the building works that the curé was thinking of undertaking. Besides, it is quite unrealistic to believe that the singer had the wherewithal... or such lavish prodigality... or that our hero was so dishonourably venal.

There is still the explanation given by the good folk of the area... the one that they will tell you and which you already suspect: Bérenger Saunière found a treasure — a treasure so fabulous that it was far from being exhausted when death took him. The most curious aspect of this whole affair is that, the more closely one looks into it, this is the only explanation which fits certain of the facts.

Even before Saunière's time, the plateau of Rennes had been the scene of some rather extraordinary discoveries: to begin with, there had been a gold ingot weighing about twenty kilos and made up of an amalgam of Arabic coins.

Then, in 1860, a bitumen-covered gold ingot of fifty kilos had been found at a place called Charbonnières, near Bézu, by a farmer called Rougé. [29]

---

[29]   Abbé Mazières, *Memoires de la Société des arts et sciences de Carcassonne, vol III, 1957-58-59.* (Author's note)

As for Saunière, he one day made the gift of a beautiful and extremely old chalice to his colleague the Abbé Grassaud, curé of Saint-Paul-de-Fenouillet (Pyrénées-Orientales), whose family still possess this piece of gold-work.

He also gave ancient coins and jewellery to several local families, who still have them: one of his *protégés,* the schoolteacher Jammes, was given enough to be able to afford to buy himself an estate.

In 1928, after Saunière's death, in a ruined hut beside the stream of Couleurs, near to Rennes-le-Château, there was found a solid gold statuette, partially melted, but with the feet still distinguishable.

This discovery links to the crucible bearing traces of molten gold which was found in the home of Saunière's family, in Montazels.

These facts help to explain his curious wanderings on the hillsides under the pretext of collecting stones; his frequent trips abroad; his contact with a bank and with a jeweller; his stubborn evasiveness when he was asked to explain the source of his sudden wealth.

However, Bérenger did one day break this silence with a half-confidence. His friend Antoine Beaux, curé of Campagne-sur-Aude, said to him half-jokingly: "To see you living in such style, old chap, one would think you'd found a treasure." He looked him straight in the eye and enunciating each word with deliberation, he answered in

Occitan: *"Me l'han donat, l'hay panat, l'hay parat é bé le téni"*. (I was shown it, I laid hands on it, I've put it somewhere safe and I'm holding on to it.")

He did not elaborate, nor did he ever mention it again, at least openly. But it is possible that he may have been making veiled and symbolic hints to it in his private journal. We have had this well-thumbed notebook in our hands and it begins in a somewhat curious fashion. The flyleaf is covered by two cuttings from the periodical *La Croix* (The Cross). The first depicts three angels bearing heavenwards a child in swaddling clothes, with the caption: "The Year 1891, borne into eternity with the fruits mentioned below." Beneath is affixed a picture of the Adoration of the Magi, captioned: "Receive, O King, gold, the symbol of royalty." These cuttings are the more surprising given that the journal itself, written in a precise and careful hand over the following pages, does not begin until May 1901 and apart from detailed information concerning the building works, contains virtually nothing of interest. But the year 1891, whose fruit was indeed golden, is precisely when Bérenger finds the documents which will make him rich... [30]

If the curé of Rennes-le-Château did indeed find a treasure, what could have been its provenance and what was it?

'Mystery' and 'Secret' are the words most frequently penned by those rare scholars who have delved into the history of the Razès and in particular of Rennes.

In his study of the most ancient inhabitants of the area, the historian R. Lizop states: "The problem posed by the mysterious oppidum of *Reddae* has never yet been properly resolved". Another historian, Louis Fédié, adds: "The origin of Rennes-le-Château is so mysterious that it seems to have deterred historians and archaeologists." In sum, as the Abbé Mazières affirms, "it is a region made famous by its legends, its traditions, its secrets, its enigmas and by a string of discoveries, some of which are sensational".

---

30   In Bérenger Saunière's personal papers we have also found this strange cryptogram:

```
Y E N S Z N U M G L N Y Y R F V H E N M Z F
P • S O T + P E C H E U R + A + L ' E M B Z
V O U C H U R E + D U + R H O N E , S O N Z
U P O I S S O N + S U R + L E + G R I L + F
L D E U X + F O I S + R E T O U R N A . U D
R N + M A L I N + S U R V I N T + E T + X H
R X V + F O I S + L E + G O U T A + . C U Z
T I T., I L + N E + L U I + R E S T A + Q V
K U E + L ' A R E T E . + U N + A N G E + T
N V E I L L A I T + E T + E N + F I T + U Q
Y N P E I G N E + D ' O R . B . S . C U R H
O V T S V K Y R M S T I J P Z C K P F X K A
```

In an attempt to shed some light on this remote corner of the world in which Bérenger lived out his extraordinary adventure, we must delve into its legends as well as its history; and these two lines of research, far from diverging, will complement each other. We shall not dismiss the legends out of hand for, whatever some simpler minds may think, they disagree with the historical facts rather less than they seem to hint at them in their own symbolic way; rather in the manner that the signs cluttering our highways can hint, to the driver who has learned to read them by following a *highway code*, of the shape of a landscape which he cannot yet see. For not only are legends often based on historical facts, which they can help us to retrace, but since the time of Marx and Freud, we know that even the most fantastical imaginings of the human mind can find their shapes and their meanings in the history of societies and even of individuals. In the face of such imaginary inventions, the historian's endeavour can — and indeed should — run parallel to that of the psychoanalyst. In approaching folklore as the latter approaches dreams, he must restore its tangible content from out of its latent and hidden meaning and lift the veil of symbols to reveal its secrets.

For both dream and legend have recourse to the same obscurantist tricks: rebus, word-play, false etymology, deliberate errors of detail, depictions of abstract ideas as people, or vice versa — and so on. By the end of this undertaking, in the same way that the analysis of dreams can distinguish episodes buried in the unconscious from those which have been deliberately suppressed, the analysis of legends can sometimes uncover facts which have been erased from the collective memory — and sometimes facts which have been intentionally hidden. In one and the same legendary motif, both procedures are often intermingled and it then becomes necessary to disentangle the attempts to reconcile different aspects of folklore, from what is a purely intellectual creation. One may then see that the fantastic can always be the means of conveying cryptically, traditions which can be linked, if only by association, to solid facts. As for the tales of the Razès in all their richness... they shed upon a yet richer history, the fleeting light of a flickering torch.

The quite remarkable nature, both of its minerals and of its water sources, ensured that people moved into the Rennes-le-Château/ Rennes-les-Bains area at a very early date. The abundance of stone, metals and metalloids which are to be found here were exploited by our ancestors throughout the ages: amber, jade, copper, lead, lead sulphide, nickel, sulphur, saltpetre, silver and gold. The seams are frequently "polar", i.e. they are oriented in relation to the magnetic meridian. Rennes-les-Bains is also on the prime Paris Meridian, which has given rise to all manner of surprising speculations.

Beneath the ramparts of Rennes-le-Château there was an ever-flowing spring. As for the springs of Rennes-les-Bains, which we have already mentioned, an old record informs us that "from time to time, mercury doth flow from the waters of the bath: therefrom may alkali be drawn, the very nitre of the alchemist; and in these waters too, may bitumen be found".

Curiously, the name Rennes, shared by the two localities of interest to us, comes from two different place-names. The name of Rennes-le-Château, once called *Aereda*, then *Reddae* or *Rhedae,* from which we have *Razès* (*Rhedesium*), derives, some say, from Aer Red, the running serpent, the Celtic or pre-Celtic god of lightning; though others suggest the Visigothic word *Rheda*, which signifies the Plough. [31] On the other hand Rennes-les-Bains, which was first called *Bains de Règnes* (the Baths of Règnes) and which, even though its springs have been known since antiquity, did not become a significant village until much later, gets its name from a composite of the Latin *Regnum* and the barbarian word *Es* or *Is*, signifying either water or stone. In this case, Rennes means either 'Royal Water' or 'Royal Stone'.

The area was inhabited very early, as can be seen from the statue of Isis and the votive inscriptions dedicated to the Mother of the Gods

---

31   Cf. The works of Louis Fédié and the Abbé Lasserre. Furthermore, an altar to Aer Red was found in the area (cf. du Mège, *Archéologie pyrénéene*, vol II, p 142). The association of the Serpent and the Plough in the name of Rennes-le-Château has not failed to produce astronomical interpretations. (Author's note)

found at Rennes-les-Bains and from the Neolithic ossuary discovered at Rennes-le-Château. And it has been continuously inhabited. After the Iberian peoples there came, at the end of the IVTH century BC, the mysterious tribe of the *Rédu,* in Latin *Redones*, which has left its name in numerous locations, such as *Camp Redon.* According to several historians, this tribe was part of the race of Belges, whose name signifies 'shepherds'. Driven from the shores of the North Sea, they divided into two groups, one of which settled in Brittany and the other in the Razès. One of the authors of the *Histoire Générale du Languedoc* notes: "It is curious to see at both ends of France that the ethnic *Redensis* and *Redones,* evidently sprung from the same root, have each arrived at the modern name of Rennes": the hypothesis of a double settlement of the *Rédu* has at least the merit of providing a satisfactory explanation of this oddity.

Later, as pointed out by an author long ago, "the Romans did settle in this land, not for the beauty thereof, for nature has favoured it but little, but because minerals of divers sort do there abound". Passing by Rennes-le-Château was the Roman road leading to Spain, which later became the road to St Jacques de Compostella: at Rennes-les-Bains the colonisers built exceedingly luxurious baths, encrusted with gold and precious stones, of which the ruins can still be seen.

This double endowment of both mines and hot springs, as well as the long history of its settlement, is reflected in local legend. From earliest times, the Pyrenees had the reputation of overflowing with precious metals. According to the Syrian chronicler, Posidonius, their name, which means the Burning Mountains, comes from a fire once lit there by shepherds: the hills burned like an immense pyre and the rocks shattered to release torrents of molten silver. When all this metal had solidified, the shepherds, realising nothing of its value, allowed it to be taken by the Phoenicians, who loaded it on to thousands of ships and in order to waste none of it, even made their anchors of silver. A curious tradition adds that this conflagration, ignited by the herdsmen, spread far to the north and halted, miraculously, at Orval, now known as Paray-le-Monial, where the Celts found sanctuary and where they raised a 'stone of witness' to the "Virgin who must bear a child". Louis Fédié reports another legend which affirms that in the caverns which once linked to the tunnels beneath the château of Rennes there has always lived a race of troglodytes, who know nothing of the course of time nor of the light of day. In addition to this faint memory of a prehistoric population, it is easy to see here the universal theme of mysterious beings who inhabit mines and who, as they wish, can either grant or deny men access.

We can likewise acknowledge in passing a female divinity familiar in Gallic mythology. Guardian of abandoned mines, tutelary lady of healing waters, grand-mother of so many of our fairies and so many of our virgins, she is the White Queen who plays so large a role in our region. Historical memories combine with the fabulous aspect of this queen, as we shall soon rediscover. But, for the moment, it is toward another group of local traditions that we must turn our attention.

"The name 'Rennes' evokes, above all, a story of gold lying abandoned in hiding places which, at the end of the last century, were rediscovered by the local priest". These are the opening lines of the remarkable book *Rennes et ses derniers Seigneurs* (Rennes and the last of its Nobility) recently written by M. René Descadeillas, curator of the library of Carcassonne. And he continues: "The first question posed by those who hear these words is — what happened in the distant past which could have been the origin of such a possibility? What sequence of events could have led to the hiding of treasures in this lonely and desolate place?" The entire historical enigma... the entire secret of Bérenger Saunière... is summed up in this question-mark.

It would seem that at Rennes, as in Bethlehem, the shepherds were the first to arrive at the grotto. Before Saunière, it was in fact a shepherd who had the dangerous privilege of laying his hands on this mysterious treasure. And as if to make the story all the more pleasing, this shepherd was called Paris. So — in the Spring of the year 1645, Ignace Paris, a young shepherd from Rennes was searching for a lost sheep. Of a sudden he heard it bleating: the animal had fallen into a pot-hole. Paris climbed down: at the bottom, a narrow passage led yet deeper. On he went and to his amazement, he reached a cavern where there were skeletons lying beside heaps of gold. Filling his cap with pieces of the precious metal, he hurried back to the village and with gold coins as proof, he told his story. But as he stubbornly refused to reveal the hiding-place, nobody would believe him. He was accused of having quite simply committed a robbery and he was stoned to death. As it stands, this story is very like a legend, but the comparisons can be misleading: for Paris, the shepherd, did indeed exist and the ruins of his house can still be seen near to Rennes.

> *Like a wretch who's stripped bare,*
> *Wild eyed and haggard,*
> *Bald of head and double horned,*
> *Bearing as his arm a halberd,*
> *At the foot of this bare hill,*
> *The angel of a bastard race,*
> *With voice abrasive and absurd,*
> *Keeps constant under watchful guard*
> *This treasure so immense in size*
> *Which, from this rock I gaze upon*
> *As if I have but hither come*
> *To mount a careful guard thereon*
> *And what it holds, that would I steal*
> *Though far he is from loosing hold.*

Replete with preposterous, if enigmatic, charm, this little poem by Labouisse-Rochefort illustrates a legend which he recounts in his *Voyage à Rennes-les-Bains*, written in 1832. At Blanchefort, the devil watches over a treasure of nineteen and a half millions — not a penny more nor a penny less. One beautifully sunny day, a shepherdess of the locality saw him counting out his gold coins on the mountainside. She immediately summoned the villagers to come to see this far from usual sight, but when they arrived the demon had once more hidden his treasure and disappeared. The villagers took counsel and went to Limoux to consult a wizard. In exchange for a decent fee and the promise of half the gold, he agreed to take on the Devil. But, he told the peasants, as soon as you hear any shouting, you must come running. This said, the *breich* [32] set off to do battle with the Evil One. And, in fact, the peasants soon heard an uproar punctuated by cries so horrible that they all took to their heels. The wizard came back, furious: "Idiots! We've lost everything — and it's all your fault. I already had hold of one string of his moneybag, but you weren't there to give me a hand." And leaving the crest-fallen peasants, he went back to Limoux. It is said that the Marquis de Fleury, Seigneur of Rennes and Blanchefort, on whose lands the incident occurred, brought an action for trespass against the villagers. It is a pity that the minutes of this case have not survived — they would certainly have lacked

---

32   An Occitan word for 'wizard'. (Author's note)

nothing of the picaresque! This detail at least helps us to assign an approximate date to the legend, as the Fleury family, of whom we shall have much more to say, did not arrive at Rennes until 1767.

Without pre-empting the criticisms called for by these two tales, we must stress that, unlike the earlier ones, they are not linked with mining folklore. The treasure to which they refer is not a gift of Nature; it is something left by the hand of man. On the other hand, guarded in the one case by skeletons and in the other by the Lord of the Nether Regions, this hoard is associated with images of the Underworld. The gold of Rennes is the Gold of the Dead.

To the legends which speak of the existence of a treasure near to Rennes, can be added various traditions concerning its origin and its nature. Firstly, it is said that Queen Blanche of Castille, driven from Paris by the Shepherds' Crusade of 1251, sought refuge in the Razès, where she had the château of Blanchefort built and where she hid her gold. When the trouble subsided, she returned to the capital and it would seem, confided the secret of the hiding place to her son, Saint Louis. He in turn would have passed it on to his own son, Philippe the Bold, who died suddenly, before he was able to pass the information on to Philippe the Fair. And so the secret of the treasure of Blanchefort was lost. According to another tradition, the château of Blanchefort takes its name from a stay which was made there by Blanche de France, daughter of Saint Louis, who is supposed to have buried a treasure not far from there.

These tales are certainly attractive with their scent of mystery but, as such, History forbids us lending them any credence. Probably founded by the Visigoths, the château of Blanchefort was the pawn in a very bitter struggle during the XIITH century. The Benedictine Abbey of Alet wanted to seize it from its lord, Bernard de Blanchefort. Pope Calixtus II personally intervened in the dispute, which he cut short in 1119 in favour of the clergy. But Bernard de Blanchefort took arms against them and after battling for eleven years, forced the Pope to back down. In 1210, during the Albigensian Crusade, Blanchefort was taken and destroyed by the French barons and was never rebuilt. [33] Neither Blanche de Castille... who was at the time only an adolescent and was not yet queen... nor Blanche de France, who was not yet even born, can therefore have stayed there. We must resign ourselves to the fact that Blanchefort and the two Queens Blanche, can only be linked together by poetic analogy.

But the legends are not confined to one Queen Blanche: that of Rennes relates to three people. The third has no treasure other than a goblet and the melancholy memory of her still hovers about the ruins of the château of

---

33   In 1238, "they of Blanchefort" are paying only one sou in tax and they are therefore, from the fiscal point of view, linked with Coustaussa (*Writ of Pierre de Voisins, from a charter of Louis VIII.*) Since this time, then, there has been neither a castle nor even a village. (Author's note)

Peyrepertuse. Guardian of the Col de La Croix in the Corbières, this imposing fortress was built by the Visigoths, then transformed in the XITH century by the house of Bézalu et Fenouillède, descendants of Béra, Count of Razès. Sheltered within its ramparts was the statue of a woman at which passers-by would hurl stones to prevent her from bewitching them. Tradition has it that there were also on the upper floors of the keep "secret doors made from a single slab, as were the tombs of the kings of Judah. These doors were fashioned of heavy stones which pivoted to lie flush in the thickness of the wall."

And so it was to this strange place that a queen of Castille named Blanche, having lived through great sorrows in her native land, had come to seek refuge. In sadness and ill-health, she spent her time in prayer and in solitary walks. One day when she had gone to drink at the fountain which flowed beneath the ramparts, her silver goblet slipped from her hands and rolled to the foot of a precipice. Centuries later it was found by a shepherd and preserved as a treasure at Caudiès in the Fenouillède, where it was still to be seen at the dawn of the French Revolution. Afflicted by the King's Evil, this Queen Blanche went one day to the baths of Rennes, when her sickness instantly vanished; this was all the more strange, as only the king of France, on the day of his crowning, had the power to cure this malady by the simple laying on of hands. Healed, the queen stayed a while longer in the Razès and then, lured by false reports, she returned to her own country and there she was put to death by her enemies.

But, it is the most ancient of the traditions of treasure at Rennes that is the most fascinating. Louis Fédié, historian of the Razès, recounts it thus: "In the Middle Ages, people believed that the precious metals extracted from the mine at Blanchefort came, not from a vein embedded in the earth, but from gold and silver ingots hidden in the vaults beneath the fortress by its earliest lords, the Visigothic kings."

Figure 4.
*Arms of the Counts of Bézalu and Fenouillède
(after L. Fédié:* History of the County of Razès
and the diocese of Alet*).*

This tradition is very curious because it runs counter to any mediaeval belief concerning mines. Our ancestors thought that metals germinated and grew in the earth like plants. In the XVITH century, Bernard Palissy was still of this opinion: "The earth," he wrote, "is never sluggard; whatever is naturally consumed within her, that doth she immediately renew."

Mines, it was believed, were like fields: the more they are worked, the more fertile do they grow. And this idea should not be surprising, as the methods of extraction produced very little and the earth beneath our feet seemed inexhaustible. With regard to such myths, stories of gold hidden in ancient mines seem not unreasonable; they are at once poetic and astute. To disguise melted gold as gold ore is, one might say, showing a certain ingenuity. And what better place to hide a treasure than in a mine which has already been explored, exploited and exhausted, where no-one will go (unless in on the secret), as everyone knows that there is no longer any metal to be found there?

Having winnowed these various traditions, we must now pass them through the sieve of criticism to see if they produce any echoes, be they even distorted or indirect, in the well-established facts of History. And to begin with, the gold of Rennes is not a myth. The existence of mines of gold and silver near to Rennes-les-Bains is mentioned in 1633 by Catel, councillor in the Parliament of Toulouse, in his *Mémoires de l'Histoire du Languedoc*. A century later, in

1734, Lamoignon de Basville, Commissioner for the Languedoc, writes: "The Romans once had gold mines in these mountains: in the rocks can be seen many openings, as well as major workings. But, whether the mines were worked out, or the art of finding them has now been lost, the treasures, if any there be, are now so hid that no-one any longer thinks to seek them out." In 1775, in his monumental *Histoire Naturelle de la Province de Languedoc*, Gensanne in his turn notes: "There was once, near to this place, considerable mining of copper, lead and silver, most especially upon the mountains of Cardou and Roquenègre, but all these workings have fallen into ruin and only some ancient debris allows us to distinguish the character of the mines once exploited there. It is the same for the mine of gold and silver that we are told had been worked on the mount of Blanchefort, a good quarter of a league below Rennes-les-Bains." And finally, in 1800, in his *Essai sur le département de l'Aude adressé au ministre de l'Intérieur* (Essay on the Aude Department, written for the Minister of the Interior), the prefect Barante refers to "two veins of silver, copper and lead in the mountains of Cardou and Roquenègre, to the north-east of Rennes-les-Bains, towards Montferrand" and "veins of gold and silver about 800 or 900 toises to the south-east of Rennes-les-Bains in the mountain of Blanchefort".

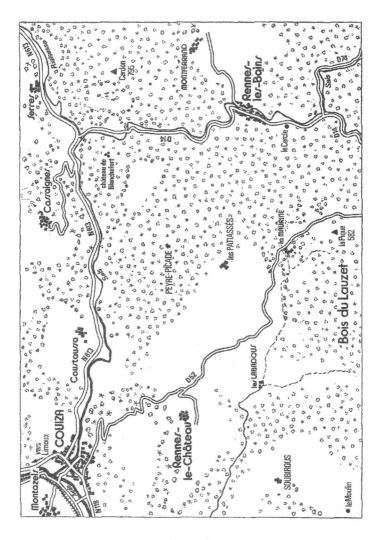

Figure 5.
The two Rennes
(1/ 75,000 scale map)

We decided to verify these statements *in situ*: the gold-bearing seam, oriented south-north and fifty metres in length, is to be found on the plots designated 625 and 626 of section A of the official land register. This seam formerly began at the surface on plot 633. However, it must be stressed that, if we are to believe Catel, all the mines of the region had been effectively exhausted since the beginning of the XVIITH century: this would explain the failure of the repeated attempts to exploit them which were undertaken between that time and the beginning of the nineteenth century.

On the 24TH of August 410, Alaric the Elder, king of the Visigoths, takes Rome and for six days sacks the city, carrying off enormous booty including the plunder taken from the Temple of Jerusalem, which had been seized by the emperor Titus in the year 70. Solomon had used more than five hundred tons of gold and silver in the construction of the Temple. In the Holy of Holies, the ritual objects: the Ark, the Seat of Mercy, the Altar of Incense, the Table of Shew-bread and the Seven-Branched Candlestick, made to the detailed instructions of Yahweh himself, formed a Holy Treasure. They could not be tampered with in any way, neither in their metal, their weight, nor their form and they were sacrosanct. In addition, the Temple held the proceeds of accumulated tribute and offerings, which were drawn upon when the State was in peril. As a result, the Temple had very often been pillaged, but the most precious treasures had never been taken, for they had been hidden in secure hiding places. Destroyed by Nebuchadnezzar, but rebuilt by Esdras, then enlarged and embellished by Herod the Great and Herod Agrippa between the year 20 and the year 64, all its former splendour had been restored when Titus took Jerusalem. The Jewish historian Flavius Josephus compares it at this time to "a sun rising above the summit of a mountain of snow". Crowning its white walls, its roof bristled with countless gold-covered spikes to keep the birds from perching there. Titus could not prevent his soldiers from setting the building ablaze, but he carried off its wealth. One can tell how much there was when one reads that when he put a part of it into circulation, the gold market in Syria immediately collapsed; which fact should give pause to those who maintain that the descriptions of the Temple are no more than the exaggerations of eastern rhetoric — if they are not purely symbolic.

Titus, however, sold only ingots and cladding tiles; the sacred objects, he took to Rome. On his triumphal arch we can still see the finest of them, such as the famous gold seven-branched candlestick, which weighed one talent (thirty-four kilos — seventy-five pounds), being carried by a slave. This treasure was first kept in the Temple of Peace and then in the Imperial Palace. It was from there, the historian Procopius tells us, that Alaric seized it.

The magnificence of the treasure of the Temple of Jerusalem fascinated all the chroniclers of antiquity and thus a number of texts allow us to follow, step by step, its vicissitudes up to the time when it was taken by Alaric. Thereafter, it is lost to History. This silence is very strange as, if such well-known and precious artefacts had later been re-taken from the Visigoths, either by the Franks or the Arabs, then everything would lead us to believe that the chroniclers would have made some mention of the fact. The Frankish historian Fredegarius and the Arab chronicler El Macin, who give detailed descriptions of the treasure of the Visigothic kings and tell us how it was taken at Toulouse by Clovis and later at Toledo by the Saracens, make no mention of anything, among the objects seized, that may have come from the Temple of Jerusalem. Some people have therefore conjectured that, being Christian, the Visigoths could hardly have failed to attach an exceptional value to the treasure of the Temple and so might well have succeeded in concealing it from the avidity of their conquerors.

In the V[TH] century, when the Visigoths make themselves masters of what later is to become the Languedoc, their State Treasure is made up of two very distinct parts: on the one hand are the tribute and the personal riches of the king, which are used for the running of the State and which are kept at Toulouse. On the other hand there is that which is called the Ancient Treasure, made up of the booty accumulated by the nation during the wandering years of conquest. This is the Holy Treasure, at once a memorial to the exploits of their ancestors and a magical surety of the power and continuity of the State. Not even the king himself is allowed to touch this, save only if the very existence of the State is in jeopardy. Apart from the spoils from the Temple of Jerusalem, this treasure consists of the Missorium, a dish of solid gold weighing five hundred pounds, which is placed upon the altar during the Mass and which Aetius had given to King Thorismond. There is also the Emerald Table, a fabulous piece of precious work, doubtless made only of glass, but which is set with three rows of pearls and supported by sixty golden feet. At the time of Alaric II, this treasure was kept at Carcassonne. In 507, after Clovis had taken Toulouse and the treasure found there, he went on to besiege Carcassonne, which was saved only by the intervention of Theodoric, king of the Italian Goths. Alaric II had been killed during this war and as his son Amalaric was a minor, Theodoric assumed the regency. Carcassonne now being vulnerable, he had the Ancient Treasure transported to Ravenna, handing it over to Amalaric when the latter became of an age to govern.

In the VIITH century, the Franks, extending their conquest, took Narbonne, where they found nothing more than sixty chalices, fifteen patens and twenty necklaces. The Visigoths had in fact taken part of the Ancient Treasure to Toledo, their Spanish capital; the Arabs laid hands on this in 711, seizing among other things the famous Missorium. What remained, comprising in particular nine solid gold votive crowns adorned with sapphires, was discovered in the nineteenth century at Guarrazar, near Toledo. These were displayed at the Cluny Museum in Paris until 1943, when Pétain gave them to Franco.[34] H.P. Heydoux, in his book *Lumières sur la Gaule* (Light upon Gaul), wrote "Shall we one day discover in France a hoard as dazzling and sumptuous as that of Guarrazar? The idea cannot be rejected".

North of the Pyrenees, the Visigothic kingdom, once so mighty, is soon reduced to the Razès. Rhedae is thus thrice powerful; from the military point of view she is key to communication with Spain and has two fortresses and four towers. From the religious point of view, she has two churches — Saint Marie and Saint John the Baptist — as well as a monastery and is angling for the status of bishopric. And her economic importance is no less — she has thirty thousand inhabitants and one of her streets can boast fourteen butcher's shops.

But that part of the Holy Treasure which neither Francs nor Arabs seem to have found...; Could it not have been confided to the wild and rugged landscape of the Razès? One can understand why there may have been those who have dreamed that Solomon's gold had been returned thus to the Pyrenean mines whence, perhaps, it had come — and that, once

---

34   The Guarrazar Treasure was later divided between France and Spain. Some objects have been stolen. What remains of the treasure was reunited for a special exhibition at the Cluny Museum in 2011. (Translator's note)

back in the bosom of its mother, it had there sucked forth a new life, sprouting, growing and multiplying like corn.

Yet certain facts endow this dream with a rather curious slant. Almost immediately after the founding of their Order, the Templars will come to the Razès, thanks to their links with two important — and turbulent — local families, the Blancheforts and the A Niorts. Between 1132 and 1137, Arnaud, Bernard and Raimond de Blanchefort make them gifts of fiefs at Pieusse, at Villarzel and at Esperaza.[35] In 1147, they establish themselves at le Bézu and at Campagne-sur-Aude on a domain ceded to them by the A Niorts. In 1156, the Order of the Templars elects a new Grand Master. And who might this be? Bertrand de Blanchefort. It is at this time that the Templars of the Razès, with the co-operation of Templars from the Rhineland, bring in from Germany a colony of workers whom they settle on the plateau of Lauzet, between Blanchefort and Rennes. The soldier-monks impose a military discipline upon these workers who are forbidden, on pain of the most severe sanctions, to have contact of any sort with the local population.[36] Special arrangements are even made to deal with their disputes: the *Judicature des Allemands* — the

---

35   *Cartulaire des Templiers de Douzens* published by Pierre Gérard & Elisabeth Magnou under the direction of Philippe Wolff, Paris, 1965. (Author's note)
36   Communication from the Abbé R.M. Mazières. (Author's note)

Court of the Germans. This segregation is explained by the very special nature of the work which they are doing. In fact, they are working the gold mine on Blanchefort.

The famous Order which had guard over the Temple of Jerusalem was unlikely, however, to get much gold from this mine which had already been exploited by the Romans: furthermore, if we are to believe the engineer César d'Arcons, who was charged in the XVIITH century with the task of investigating the mines of the region, the Germans employed in this work were smelters, rather than miners. This makes it easier to understand the most ancient tradition of the gold of Rennes, according to which this gold came, not from a mine, but from a hoard of Visigothic origin.

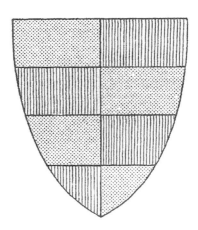

Figure 6.
Arms of Bertrand de Blanchefort, Grand Master of the Order of the Temple in 1156. Checkered or and gules eight times. (*Source: M. Métraux:* The Blancheforts and the origins of the feudal lordship of Guyenne.)
Whether he was French or Occitan, a Herald at Arms spells these arms out as: "The gold of Rennes escaped him."

A century after ceding le Bézu and Campagne-sur-Aude to the Templars, we again encounter the A Niort family... this time upon the same historical scene as Blanche de Castille, one of the heroines of the legends of the gold of Rennes.

This was at the time of the Albigensian Crusade. Two generations of the Seigneurs d'A Niort, ardent followers of the Cathare faith, distinguished themselves under the banner of Toulouse against Simon de Montfort and Pierre de Voisins, his seneschal for the Razès. Simon had richly endowed Pierre with lands, at the expense of the Blancheforts and the A Niorts, giving him Rennes, Blanchefort and Campagne in 1215. But the A Niorts, shrewd politicians, had a foot in both camps and well enough to ensure that even the Pope could not get the better of them. It was only by appealing to the Regent of France, Blanche de Castille, that in 1237 he succeeded in having them condemned as heretics by a tribunal — of which Pierre de Voisins was a member. Condemned to death or life imprisonment, with the confiscation of their goods confirmed, the A Niort, contrary to all expectation, were nevertheless released not long after and regained part of their lands.

In 1243, independent Occitania is on the point of death but Montségur, the last Cathare bastion, still stands defiant. "The dragon's head must be lopped," Blanche of Castille is supposed to have said. And she did indeed seem to be possessed by an unwonted passion to take the fortress, which her Catholic zeal does not suffice to explain. So did Blanche come to Occitania, as the legend would have it? We cannot tell, but she followed events day by day. In the autumn of 1243, after five months of siege, the situation for the defenders of Montségur is growing worse and they are forced to consider negotiation — an uncomfortable prospect for, it would seem, they can hope for little mercy. Indeed, Pierre-Roger de Mirepoix, commander of the place, as well as a great number of the defenders are not only "harbourers of heretics", but a year earlier they had murdered eleven inquisitors at Avignonet. Moreover, the Count of Toulouse, Raimond VII, whose final attempt at insurrection has just failed, is seeking to make peace with the Pope and has just, albeit reluctantly, agreed to give up Montségur.

At this moment, a man appears who is going to engage in some mysterious dealings: this is Ramon d'A Niort. He is the son-in-law of Pierre-Roger de Mirepoix, the brother-in-law of the Seigneur de Montségur, Ramon de Perelha. He has the ear of Raimond VII and doubtless it is Blanche of Castille who was responsible for his acquittal in the previous year. At Christmas 1243, he sends an emissary named Escot de Belcaire to Montségur who, after slipping through the besieging army, reaches the castle to deliver letters to Pierre-Roger. He tells him that a fire will be lit on the nearby mountain of Bidorta "if the Count of Toulouse manages things well". After which the messenger departs and on the following night there is indeed a light upon the mountain-top. A few days later two heretics, Mattheus and Pierre Bonnet, succeed in slipping away from the besieged castle, carrying "gold, silver and a great amount of money," which they are to hide for the time being in a fortified cavern.

Fernand Niel writes, "This introduces two characters whose actions, given the circumstances, give pause for thought: the Count of Toulouse and Ramon d'A Niort. The defenders of Montségur would doubtless have found it in somewhat questionable taste to have sent a messenger who has nothing more to say than that the Count of Toulouse was managing his affairs well, unless these 'affairs' had something to do with the fate of the garrison. In addition, one cannot see Escot de Belcaire climbing Bidorta and lighting a fire on the summit to confirm what he had come to say two days previously. The most logical sense in his mission must therefore lie in secret transactions being carried on between Pierre-Roger de Mirepoix and some other person on the outside. But who was this person?"

On the 1ST of March 1244, the defenders of Montségur asked to negotiate. The conditions which they were offered were beyond their hopes. Not only would they be able to leave with arms, baggage and the honours of war, (with the exception of those heretics who, should they refuse to abjure, would be consigned to the flames), they would even be absolved of the murder of the inquisitors. Furthermore, they were granted the right to remain in the castle for two weeks. On the 13TH of March, the night preceding the surrender, three Cathares, Hugo, Poitevin and Amiel Aicard, slipped away from the castle, dangling from ropes down the length of the rocky and precipitous mountainside. "And this was done lest the Church of the heretics should lose its treasure which was hid in the forests and whereof the fugitives knew the hiding place." [37]

In allowing these three men to escape, Pierre-Roger de Mirepoix was violating the clause in the surrender agreement which obliged him to hand over all recalcitrant heretics; he was thereby taking the risk of condemning to death all — himself included — who had just, against all expectation, been granted life and liberty. M. Niel wonders: "What, then, could this treasure have been that it had to be saved at all costs? It pleases us to think that the fugitives were not saving a material treasure: had this not already been removed two months earlier by Mattheus and Pierre Bonnet? This time, we believe, it was a question of objects of much greater value, of a spiritual treasure, perhaps parchments, on which were recorded the secrets of a religion which saved its adherents from the fear of death by fire."

---

[37]   Statement of Arnaud-Roger de Mirepoix *in* Doat, vol XXII, p.129. (Author's note)

Another hypothesis has been suggested: that Blanche of Castille only achieved the surrender of Montségur in exchange for highly important genealogical documents which the defenders of the castle, once these were in their hands, would have concealed in a safe place. Were these the letters handed over by Ramon d'A Niort's messenger? Were these what the fugitives took with them on that last night? These which, according to what some people now claim, were rediscovered much later and then hidden away? We will probably never know: the surrender of Montségur keeps its mystery, as the defenders were no longer in a position to make demands, nor did their adversaries have any reason to make them a gift without something in return.

Pierre-Roger de Mirepoix ends his days a free man. Pierre de Voisins, in 1244, is obliged to hand Campagne over to the Templars. In 1247, he must also cede a number of estates to Ramon d'A Niort, as Louis IX had received this dubious character at court and had agreed to his demands — as one does for a man who needs to be treated with circumspection.

In 1269, Blanche de France, daughter of Louis IX, marries Ferdinand, heir to the throne of Castille. He is known as the *Infant de la Cerda,* which means the 'Son of the Sow', because on his shoulder he had a thick tuft of hair, like the bristles of a hog. Six years later, Ferdinand dies before his father, leaving two sons, Alfonso and Ferdinand. Sancho, younger brother of the deceased, then seizes the two children, has himself proclaimed king and sends Blanche into exile. She crosses the mountains and in 1280 comes to the Razès; not, as legend would have it, to Blanchefort, which was already destroyed, but to Rennes, where she stays with its lord, Paul de Voisins.[38] She brings with her substantial funds to pay the army which she intends to raise to free and to restore the young Alfonso, who thereafter is known as *El Desdichado*, 'The Disinherited'.

Her plan enjoyed a threefold backing: that of her brother, Philippe III the Bold, King of France — of King James I of Majorca — and of the Templars. In fact, James I of Majorca has just become engaged in a conflict with his brother, Pedro III of Aragon. On the other side of the Pyrenees, then, there are two factions, the Aragonese and the Majorcans. The King of France and the Templars support Majorca; the former, to put and end to the traditional Aragonese claims upon the Languedoc and the latter, because the kingdom of Majorca was their creation and their fief — and the King of Aragon has been subjecting them to a series of political humiliations. The three kings meet at Toulouse in 1280. Pedro III agrees to seize the 'Children of the Cerda' from Sancho, but this proves to be in order to lay hands on them himself, upon which he states his intention of not returning them to

---

38   Younger son of Pierre I de Voisins. (Author's note)

their mother without receiving the Carcassès [39] and the Razès in exchange. At the same time, midst the intrigues surrounding the children, a decisive phase in the unity of Spain is being played out. In fact, King Alfonso X, grandfather of *El Desdichado*, proposes the breaking-up of his dominions in order to give his grandson the kingdom of Jaén. [40] But the Cortès, who are opposed to this dismemberment of the kingdom, depose him, at which he appeals for help to the Sultan of Morocco. Sancho then fights off the Sultan, thus giving the appearance of being the champion of national independence. He is proclaimed king in 1284. As one can see, this game is being played for high stakes. After years of negotiation, *El Desdichado* ends by renouncing his rights in exchange for the sum of five hundred thousand gold *maravédis,* to be paid to him in the form of an annuity. But one of these precious consignments never arrives: it had been attacked *en route* and word spread that the theft was the work of Paul de Voisins, Seigneur of Rennes, who was obliged to lay low for a while. *El Desdichado* settles in the Languedoc, where he becomes Seigneur of

---

39   The Carcassès is the region to the south of Carcassonne, of which it is the principal city. (Translator's note)

40   Jaén is part of Andalusia in the south of Spain. (Translator's note)

Lunel and founds a family. [41]

Figure 7.
Arms of the House of VoisinsArgent, three lozenges gules, two and oneThe Occitans were unable to resist making an impolite play with words on the "lozenged" (diamond-shaped) shield of theNorthern Barons who were imposed upon them by Simon deMontfort

In August 1283, Philippe III the Bold makes a discreet visit to the Razès. He is accompanied by his son, the future Philippe le Bel, then aged fifteen. Where do the King and the Crown Prince go? Firstly to stay with the Templars at Campagne-sur-Aude and then with the A Niorts at Brenac. During this visit Prince Philippe who was, it should be said, coldness itself, formed a close friendship with Ramon and Udaut, the two young lords of A Niort. [42] It would seem that it

---

41   Lunel is the only town in France which is said to have been founded by the Hebrews. In any case, the Jews had been settled there since before the Roman conquest and the town has an ancient synagogue. Its coat-of-arms bears a crescent moon and its inhabitants are known as 'The Fishers of the Moon'. (Author's note)
42   Archive of the Abbé M.R. Mazières. (Author's note)

was this journey that gave rise to the legend that Philippe III had learned something from his father of a "secret of Rennes"... that he had put the last pieces together *in situ* and then died before he could pass it on to Philippe le Bel.

In 1285, Philippe the Bold dies. Philippe IV le Bel ascends the throne and his young friend Udaut d'A Niort is received into the Templar Order at Campagne. On Friday the thirteenth of October 1307, all the Templars throughout the kingdom of France are arrested. A drama now ensues whose protagonists are well-known to everyone in France from their schooldays: the King Philippe le Bel — the Grand Master Jacques de Molay — and the Pope Clement V, who was born Bertrand de Goth. What is less well-known is that the latter, by his mother Ida de Blanchefort, was grand-nephew of Bertrand de Blanchefort, Grand Master of the Templars who, a century and a half before, had employed the famous German metal-workers to explore the mines on his family lands. Another fact well worth noting: none of the Templars of le Bézu were arrested.

In 1310, Philippe le Bel sends his chamberlain, Enguerrand de Marigny to the Razès, with the task of laying hands on all the remaining possessions of the Templars. On the whole, he succeeded but, strangely, he was able to seize nothing from the Templars of le Bézu. Five years later, Marigny was summarily hanged after a dubious trial. In 1319, thirteen of the Roussillon Templars disappeared mysteriously, one by one. Perhaps the Templars of le Bézu had been able to prove that they did not actually own, but were merely the guardians of the funds which were found there. Perhaps the actual owners themselves made this claim. Perhaps, finally, the king's agents were able to find nothing because everything had been very well hidden. We must not forget that, at le Bézu, the Templars were on Voisin land. Was it they who tucked away for themselves, the riches which were in danger of being confiscated? This seems quite likely, if one is to judge by the events which were to unfold at le Bézu thirty years later.

In 1340, agents of the royal seneschal appear at the château of le Bézu to arrest two knights, Guilhem Catala and Pierre de Palajan de Coustaussa. They have, in fact, been found guilty of the crime that "... many times, at le Bézu and elsewhere, they did smelt and strike false money", with the complicity of two women, Agnès Mayssène, of Caderone and Brunissende de Gureyo. Caught in the act, the culprits waste no time in prevarication: they quickly despatch 'to join his fore-fathers', Guillaume Servin, one of the men who have come to unmask them. Little is known of Pierre de Palajan or Agnès Mayssène. On the other hand, Guilhem Catala was not a 'nobody': he was the nephew of Jacques Fournier, otherwise known as Benedict XII, the current Pope. He was also the son-in-law of the Seigneur of Rennes, Jacques de Voisins, whose wife was none other than Brunissende de Gureyo. Four years later, the culprits are pardoned.

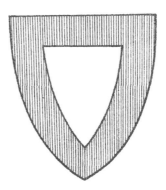

Figure 8.
Arms of Pope Bendict XII:
Argent with an orle gules.
The Herald at Arms reads this as:
The silver and the gold are near to Rennes

Striking 'false money', at this time, could have two distinct meanings: it was either to put into circulation spurious coins containing less precious metal than was required by law, or it was to strike coins of a good quality, but without the authority to issue them. Now, at the time when this affair is taking place, nobody any longer had the right to strike money "save by authorisation of the Sovereign Pontiff, or of another sovereign". Did the Voisins, who owed their rise to the Montforts, strike their "false money" with the consent of Philippe VI de Valois, King of France, who at the time was supporting Jean de Montfort against the English in his claim to the succession to Brittany? This is unlikely as, if this were the case, why would they have been pursued by officials of the central authority? Did Guilhem Catala do it with the blessing of his uncle the Pope? It is possible that, from this time, the Holy See may have begun to take an interest in the gold of Rennes. But, whatever the case may be, in order to strike money one must have the necessary metal. Whence, then, came that which the Voisins were turning into hard cash? And why would they have taken such enormous risks when they could simply have sold the metal? Without doubt it is because, for one reason or another, the provenance and the working of this metal had to be concealed. In other words, the fabrication of the false money of le Bézu provided a solution to the same problem which was to face Bérenger Saunière so many years later: how to cash in on a treasure without immediately revealing its existence? There is only one answer to this problem: melt down the metal.

In 1352, the young King of Aragon and Castille, Pedro I, who is soon to be dubbed 'The Cruel', marries Blanche de Bourbon, sister-in-law to the Dauphin of France, the future Charles V. This political marriage has been forced upon the young prince by his mother, but he is enamoured of the beautiful Jeanne de Castro. Unlike many another, Pedro is unwilling to accept his fate... not even in appearance. Barely three days after the marriage, he shuts Blanche up in a convent in Medina and then, despite all protests, he lives openly with the woman of his choice. Using his misconduct as a pretext, the Queen Mother incites his two brothers, Sancho and Henri de Trastamare, against him. But the plot fails and in 1361, Trastamare flees to France, taking with him his feared Aragonese mercenaries and there he lays siege to Rennes-le-Château. The lower town no longer existed — it had already been destroyed two centuries before in a raid by the *Aragous*. But the Voisins have rebuilt the fortifications of the upper city, as befitting the chief town of their considerable estates. The mercenaries ransack the monastery, then their artillery bombards the tower containing the powder magazine. The explosion blows a breach in the rampart, which they surge through. Then, stone by stone, they set about demolishing the church of St John the Baptist. Tradition has it that they were hunting for something valuable which was hidden there. It adds that the church was booby-trapped and a pivoting stone hurled fifteen of the too-curious assailants into a tunnel and bones were broken. The end comes in pillage, destruction and massacre, to be compounded by a plague. From this day on, opulent Rennes will be no more than a village.

To silence the scandal-mongers, Pedro the Cruel claims that his wife has been unfaithful to him with his own brother, Frederic. He has him executed. [43] As for poor Blanche, she is to die in 1362, murdered in her prison either by poison, or like Desdemona, suffocated beneath her pillow.

---

43   Blanche is supposed to have had a son by Frederic, Don Enrique, founder of the Enriquez family, who were in fact supposedly closely linked to the House of Castille, though in quite what way is uncertain. (Author's note)

Be all this as it may, the Pope and the King of France support the claim of Trastamare to the throne of Castille. The pretender returns across the mountains with his mercenaries, aided by du Guesclin, [44] who has recruited for this campaign a number of Occitan lords, whose families were Cathares who had been ruined during the crusade. Pedro is forced to flee and Trastamare is proclaimed king. But his victory is short-lived. Supported by the English troops of the Black Prince, Pedro defeats his rival. Once again Trastamare takes refuge in France, but his mercenaries are far from forgotten and he gets a very cool reception. All that the King will grant him is asylum in the château of Peyrepertuse, where he will live for a number of years with his wife, Jeanne de Penafiel and their children.

And so we have the melancholy Queen of Castille who comes to Peyrepertuse...

To weep like Diana beside these same springs
Her love in its solitude ever in peril...

nor was her name Blanche, but Jeanne. And thus does it often come about that folk memory blends into one, the several personalities who are connected to the same place, or to the same events. Jeanne de Trastamare has been

---

44   Bertrand du Guesclin (c 1320-1380) was Constable of France and a famous and highly successful military commander. He died on campaign in the Languedoc. (Translator's note)

conveniently endowed with the name and the touching sorrows of Blanche de Bourbon and doubtless also those of Blanche de France.

But here, History seems to take a mischievous delight in playing with myth. The Cathare knights who accompanied du Guesclin to Castille were called the *Moundis*, which means the Pure Ones. To the common folk, they were known as *la Gent Blanco,* the White People... to their foes, the White Company, as they wore upon their jerkins the white cross which is later to become the cross of the Armagnac faction. Finally, it is near to the frontier with Aragon, in a "White Castle" which can be located nowhere else, that du Guesclin rejoins Trastamare:

> *To the White Castel did King Henri straight go*
> *Which of his heritage, by right did he own...*

From this delving into History, into legend and into their mutual connections, one may draw certain conclusions:

1 - Since the Middle Ages there has been the tradition of a treasure, or several treasures in turn, which have been hidden near to Rennes.

2 - This tradition is not so absurd, as it is corroborated by some well-established facts as well as some probabilities: the (probable) existence of a Visigothic treasure at Carcassonne; the existence of a gold mine at Blanchefort; the working of this mine in the

Middle Ages; the (probable) repository of the funds of the Majorcan faction; the striking of counterfeit money at le Bézu; the discovery of a considerable amount of melted gold in the XIXTH century.

3 - Nevertheless, there is no convincing early document which can enable us to move from hypothesis to certainty.

If we now consider the tradition in its mythic form, its content is far more instructive:

The gold of Rennes is presented to us as an incalculable hoard, of mysterious origin, which has played — or is destined to play — a role of great political importance and having more than one owner: the State, the Church, a religious Order or party. This gold appears most often associated with the theme of plunder: the Cathare Church, the "rebellious" families such as the A Niorts, Blanche de Bourbon, the Templars, El Desdichado. In every case it is concerned with people of title, whose legitimate rights have been violated, be they rights of inheritance, or rights of blood.

Furthermore, the various versions of the tradition, which are contradictory in an historical sense, converge mythologically. It matters little, from a thematic point of view, that the treasure may be linked sometimes to Blanche de Castille, mother of Louis IX, sometimes to Blanche de Bourbon, Queen of Castille; whether it be located sometimes at Blanchefort or sometimes at le Bézu. In fact, the ancient name of le Bézu, *Albedunum,* translates precisely as Blanchefort. The treasure, in a very poetical sense, thus shares the ubiquity of the "White Castle" in which it is protected. And just as the analysis of a dream can often bring out the name of a place hidden behind that of a person, here Blanche de Castille may well be a simple metaphor for *Castillo Blanco*, the White Castle. Finally, at le Bézu, as at Blanchefort, the treasure belongs to the "*Blancs*" — the 'White Ones': the Albigensians, the White Mantles, or the White Queens. And to make this whiteness yet more dazzling, the legend, using landscapes or events with great artistry, makes it stand out against a black background: this is Blanchefort against Roco Negro, Rennes on its mountain against Rennes in the valley, the White King against the Black King, the Devil against the Shepherdess. This bi-polarity — according to which way one's thoughts and fantasies may turn — is a reflexion of the Baucent, the enigmatic black and white standard of the Templars; of a chessboard, at once theatre of war and frame for a puzzle; of the domino which is both game and disguise; in short of anything which symbolises an indissoluble unity of opposites, those of plain intelligence and the imaginings of the night. It is thus, in its metaphysical contradictions, that legend weaves its spell.

Yet again, the gold of Rennes is, from its very beginnings, the gold of the Dead. The gold of the Visigothic kings, who were buried with their treasure; the gold of the Cathares or the

Templars, who were cast into the flames; the gold of queens, lying dead in their prison cells; the gold watched over by the Prince of Darkness, or by skeletons.

After all, this gold has been seen by no-one save some young shepherds, symbols of innocence. This final element in the theme of legend is all the more interesting as the popular imagination is fired by it, to transmute hidden gold into spiritual treasure.

In this respect, Bérenger Saunière is an exception. Certainly, he too was a shepherd to his flock, but he had early lost the innocence of childhood and now trailed a whiff of sulphur and once he had found the gold of the Dead he could not restrain himself, with the ferocity of guilt, from effacing a tomb inscription which evoked the innocence of Arcadia...

But we are not yet altogether finished with the mythology of Rennes. It is under this heading that, not having been able to dissipate the uncertainties which colour their sources and their intent, we must list two very strange works published recently in Geneva, in very limited editions and whose authors hide themselves behind what are evidently symbolic pseudonyms. The first appeared in 1956, with the signature Henri Lobineau and is entitled: *Genealogy of the Merovingian Kings and origins of various French and foreign families of Merovingian descent according to the Abbé Pichon, Doctor Hervé and the parchments of the Abbé Saunière, of Rennes-*

le-Château (Aude). [45] The second, published in 1963, is titled: *The Merovingian descent or the Enigma of Razès of the Visigoths,* [46] signed by Madeleine Blancasall, translated from the German by Walter Celse-Nazaire.

The thesis proposed in these two works is, to say the least, astonishing. According to their authors, the line of the last Merovingian King, St Dagobert II — who was assassinated in the Forest of Woëvre, near Stenay on 23RD December 679 — did not die with him. In fact, his son, Sigebert IV, (who according to most historians was murdered with his father), supposedly took refuge at Rhedae and adopted the title of Count of Razès. There he founded a family, died and in 758 was buried in the church, beneath the tombstone now called *la Dalle du Chevalier* (the Knight's Stone). It is this Sigebert IV who is said to have had the image of his father carved upon the menhir called the *Cap de l'Homme* (the Man's Head), near to Rennes which is locally often held to be that of St Dagobert.

Nothing is so obscure and so little known as the history of the last of the Merovingians. Like their extraordinary beginning, the disappearance of their dynasty is shrouded in mystery. This

---

45   *Généalogie des rois mérovingiens et origines des diverses familles françaises et étrangères de souche mérovingienne d'après l'abbé Pichon, le docteur Hervé et les parchemins de l'abbé Saunière, de Rennes-le-Château (Aude).*
46   *Les descendants mérovingiens ou l'Enigme du Razès wisigoth.*

is a time of drama: of murders, of rapes, of substituted children, of kings who are proclaimed, deposed and suddenly reappear, of convoluted genealogies. Specialists have recently brought to light the relations between the country of the Aude and the Rhine-Meuse region, starting-point for the rise of the Merovingians. The discovery in Merovingian graveyards, in Lorraine and also near to Castelnaudary, of ritually pierced skulls, has demonstrated this affinity. The study of place-names already gives a hint: as, in the Aude *Issel* and *la Sals* reflect *Issel* and *la Sala* in Guelderland, from whence came the Salian Franks. Whatever the case, thanks to modern writers, the multi-faceted treasure of Rennes is being enriched with a new dimension: it is no longer simply hidden gold, but a hidden bloodline. It has become the treasure of a dynasty and is reawakening a myth whose political purpose, throughout the history of the French nation, has been far from insignificant. This is the myth of the Lost King.

*
* *

From the XVTH century onwards, the Razès seems to have forgotten its venturesome past. This can now scarcely even be glimpsed, apart from in the misted looking-glass of tradition. The very earth itself seems, little by little, to be casting a dense mantle of brambled growth upon its ancient secrets. But all about this earth, alliances, intrigues and covetousness continue to entwine themselves. Even today they are at work.

The House of Hautpoul was one of the most ancient and most illustrious of the Land of Oc. Its founding fathers were called the Kings of the Black Mountain, for it was there that their birthplace lay and there that they held mines — among others, the gold-mine of Salsines. The Hautpouls are to be found at the Crusades, then in the Albigensian war, on the side of the South. In 1422, they form an alliance with the Voisin family, the Seigneurs of Rennes and in 1732 François d'Hautpoul marries Marie de Négri d'Ables whose mysterious tombstone we have already encountered.

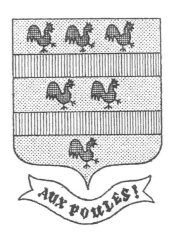

Figure 9.
Arms of the House of Hautpoul:
Or, twice-banded gules, charged with six cocks, sable, 3, 2, 1.
Motto: "Aux Poules!" (A play with words: 'poule' = cock)
The Herald at Arms interprets this as 'the gold of the Goths
was at Rennes, and women tookpossession of it'.

But the trees, even genealogical ones, must not prevent us from seeing the wood. From these somewhat boring alliances let us simply hold on to this: from the XVTH century onward, all the lands where the strange events through which we have guided the reader have been played out, are consistently held in the same hands. From the Voisins they passed to the Hautpoul-Blancheforts, then to the Fleurys... three names which were finally to become one.

In 1644, François-Pierre d'Hautpoul, Baron de Rennes, had made his will, attaching to it the archives which, from the XITH century on, were proof of the transmission of the fiefs and titles which he held. These documents were registered at Esperaza, on 23RD November, with M. Captier, the public notary. But when the Baron d'Hautpoul died, his heirs were unable to examine either the will or the documents: everything had mysteriously disappeared.

This is also the time when the royal authorities are showing a renewed interest in the mines of the Razès. The Comptroller de Basville writes: "Monsieur Colbert fits out a company in 1692 to work these mines: he even brings people from Sweden into the scheme, but his efforts produce only the discovery of a few veins of copper, which soon run out and which are far from covering the expense of the find." [47]

---

47   Jean-Baptiste Colbert followed Nicolas Fouquet as Minister of Finance to Louis XIV. The author gives the date 1692 in this quotation — though Colbert died in 1683. (Translator's note)

In 1695, Henri d'Hautpoul, Baron de Rennes, the grandson of François-Pierre, dies. He leaves four sons, Blaise, Charles, François and Joseph. He also leaves his will. But, contrary to the right of the first-born which was enshrined in law, it is François who, even though he is third in line, takes over the château of Rennes, takes over the management of the ancestral lands and takes, as we have seen, the extraordinary title of Marquis de Blanchefort. Better still, he holds on to the paternal will, which for the next forty-eight years, he will refuse to let anyone see. To this assemblage of anomalies one can add another, yet more astonishing: not a single voice in the family is raised in protest.

In 1780, a hundred and thirty years after its mysterious disappearance, the will of François-Pierre d'Hautpoul reappears no less mysteriously with another Esperaza notary, Jean-Baptiste Siau. Hearing of this, Pierre d'Hautpoul, Seigneur of Serres, naturally asks for access to it. But he receives from the notary, in writing, this surprising response: "It would be imprudent of me to release a will of such great importance." Upon which the documents once more disappear. M. Descadeillas, in his *Rennes et ses derniers seigneurs* (Rennes and its last Lords) wonders: "What has become of this document? One may search for it in vain today, for it was confirmed that the original was being held and therefore no copy ever figured in the archive of the notary who had charge of it. But it could free us from the uncertainty which will long continue to hover over many details in the genealogy of the Hautpouls." [48]

Figure 10.
Arms of the House of Negre d'Ables:
Azure charged at its heart with a right gauntlet argent,
armed,dexter a stag passant and sinister a hare passant
each of the like.

In fact, in December 1780, the notary Siau had handed these significant papers to Marie de Négri d'Ables, widow of François d'Hautpoul-Blanchefort. And in January 1781 she had entrusted them to the Abbé Antoine Bigou, curé of Rennes-le-Château who was also

---

48   René Descadeillas, *op.cit.* The original here in question is probably the confirmatory document provided by the Intendant de Bezons on 4 January 1664. (Author's note)

her chaplain. [49] When in her turn, Marie de Négri d'Ables died, custom required that the family papers be handed over to her older daughter Marie so that they should pass to the Hautpoul-Félines. But these papers, or at least some of them, remained in the hands of Elisabeth, the younger and unmarried child. Badgered with requests and even with court actions by her sisters and brothers-in-law, she steadfastly refused to turn them all over. She insisted that it was necessary "to *decipher* and to clarify what the family title was — and what it was not". She made the excuse that she could not open the coffers for fear that one of the precious documents might go missing.

Nor can we attempt to explain why the Blanchefort title passed, not to Marie, the eldest daughter of François d'Hautpoul, who had married her cousin, Hautpoul-Félines, but to the youngest of the sisters, Gabrielle, who revived it through her husband, Paul-François-Vincent de Fleury.

By this marriage, this latter had inherited the mines of Roco Negro and Cardou, close to Rennes. But then, in 1782, a certain Dubosc, from Rouen, arrives at Rennes and seeking no authorisation from the Marquis de Fleury,

---

[49]   In March 1781 Antoine Bigou was asked by the famous *juge d'armes*, Hugues d'Hozier de Sérigny for access to these papers in order to establish a brevet. This was delivered on 30 April 1781 (Author's note). A 'juge d'armes' was an officer corresponding to a king-of-arms of the College of Arms in England. (Translator's note)

reopens these mines. When Fleury objects, Dubosc, who already had the concession to work other mines in the region, claims that he is acting by virtue of an order from the King who has granted him the right of exploitation. And in fact the Languedoc Administration upholds his claim. Yet again, there is a law-suit. This ends in success for the Marquis de Fleury who is granted the concession in his own right. But, by now, it is 1789... [50]

So many vanishing wills, so much mystery, so much litigation can lead one to think that there was, in fact, some secret "of great importance" in the Hautpoul family. Was it the secret of a precious hoard? Of a family descent which it was impossible to reveal? Or perhaps both? In any case, if there were a secret, its last legitimate possessors could only have been Marie de Négri d'Ables, her daughter Elisabeth and their chaplain Antoine Bigou.

Marie de Négri d'Ables, Dame d'Hautpoul de Blanchefort died in her château at Rennes at the age of sixty-seven years, on the 17TH January 1781 — at least, if we are to believe her epitaph. The epitaph which the Abbé Antoine Bigou took as much care in composing as Bérenger Saunière took, a century later, in effacing it. In reading this strange text, it is surprising to learn that he spent two years over the creation of an inscription which seems to make no obvious

---

50   ... And the beginning of the French Revolution. (Translator's note)

sense and of which every line includes a mistake or anomaly and where the very names of so illustrious a lady have twice been fudged.

In August 1792, the Abbé Bigou refused to take the oath of allegiance to the new French Republic. In September of the same year he emigrated clandestinely to Sabadell in Spain, at the same time as Mgr de la Cropte de Chanterac, Bishop of Alet, and the Abbé Cauneilles, curé of Rennes-les-Bains as well as several other priests. He died two years later.

The Marquis de Fleury also took the road into exile. It is thought to be he who, before leaving, had another stone carved which was later to be found, by chance, buried beneath a holly oak, lost once more and then rediscovered in 1928 hidden in a cleft in a rock on the mountain of Coumesourde, near to Rennes-les-Bains. This, too, is a strange stone.

Figure 11.
Arms of the House of Fleury:Azure with, ground of gold, and above a band of sable ermine with dexter and sinister three crescents argent unaligned,the upper upwards, the two others back to back with, at its point, a triple-towered castle joined by a curtain wall picked out with sable.

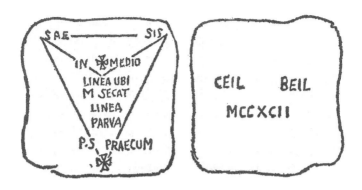

Figure 12.
The Coumesourde Stone (copied by Ernest Gros).

"Where History is mute, the stones speak" is a proverb dear to archaeologists. At Rennes the stones speak cryptically. It would seem that they said far too much for the liking of some, as there are those who have persisted — and still persist — in attempting to silence them forever... both the stones and those who have learned their secrets.

On the plateau, at Rennes, the ruins of Blanchefort against Roco Negro.

Rennes-les-Bains and the high eagle's nest of Cardou, rich in kaolin.

Rennes-le-Château, today a village of a few houses, once the capital of a powerful kingdom.

Bérenger Saunière

Emma Calvé

Mgr Billard

Marie Denarnaud

Et in Arcadia Ego: NICOLAS POUSSIN,
Les Bergers d'Arcadie.
(*Louvre Museum*)

MISSION
189·

In this Visigothic pillar, parchments …

Rennes-le-Château Church: the stone known as 'Of The Knight',
today in the Museum of Carcassonne.

Bérenger Saunière: a strange page from his journal

Rennes-le-Château: the Magdala Tower

Rennes-le-Château: the orangerie

Rennes-le-Château: verandas and gardens

Rennes-le-Château: villa Béthanie

Rennes-le-Château: château of the Voisins,
Hautpoul-Blanchefort and Fleury families

The tomb of Bérenger Saunière at Rennes-le-Château: the excavation visible in front of this tomb made in 1966 by local inhabitants. Attempting to dig?

The macabre excavation of 1956: the corpses of three men, shot. Bones, traces of flesh ... (Photo Rougé)

Compte des travaux et fournitures de
Mr Charles Denarnaud

1894 - Juillet   Porte du Cimetière

une serrure	2 1/4 kil	à 90	192	60
deux poignées		4,00	7	
deux tôles émaillées		4,06	6	
deux bordures nickelées		4,06	6	60
deux serrures de bronze		1,75	3	50
deux colin porte-champ		1,75	3	50
Porte de la cour			1	60
Pavillon	36 kilo	0,70	25	40
un autre porte de la cour	56 kilo	0,60	33	60
un autre pour treille	8 kilo	0,60	4	80
douze barres rondings	4 k 50	0,60	2	40
	45 kilo	0,60	27	60
vingt chevilles				
un paquet fil de fer fin	1 kilo	0,60	1	00
un paquet fil de fer gros	2 kilo	0,80	2	00
30 mètres de grillage	5 kilo	0,70		
4 mètres de grillage		0,85	· 7	
3 mètres de grillage		0,65	2	60
2 bancs en fonte		0,45	4	35
une pile manchin		22	44	
botte Ceruse			3	
deux paquets d'œillet	5 kilo	0,80	4	
quatre paquet dorure		0,70	1	40
vernis pour dorure		0,80		
noir de vigne			1	20
quatre pinceaux		0,85	0	25
			1	10

nov.	2	1 voyage bois et barrot fumier 2 paires de b. 2 personnes
	2	1 voyage barrot fumier . 3 attelage . 2 personnes
	3	1 voyage barrot . echauffaudage . 2 attelage . 2 personnes
	5	1 voyage bois en echauffaudage ; 2 attelage . 2 personnes
	7	1 voyage glatté 22 sacs chez Castel 2 attelage 2 personnes
	9	1 voyage barrot et 3 balles engrais . 2 attelage 2 hommes
	11	1 voyage table ... 2 attelage 2 personnes
	16	1 voyage glatté 22 sacs chez Castel 2 attelage 2 personnes
Dec.	3	1 voyage glatté 15 sacs chez Castel . 2 attelage 2 personnes
Janvier		1 transport du seul premier détail de 1 stère 600 ...
	8	1 voyage barrot ferrure, menuiserie etc. 2 attelage 2 personnes
	10	1 voyage chorée, 10 sacs plâtre, 10 sacs chaux, 5 sacs ciment, 2 attelage ...
	16	1 voyage chaux (10 sacs Delongey) 2 portes, filets, et divers (1 attel. 2 hom
	17	1 voyage table (2 attelage 2 personnes)
	22	1 voyage table, barrot, étrier, tuile, gaine, courant, etc. 2 attell. 2 h
	26	1 voy. 25 sacs de glatté chez Castel (2 attelage 2 personnes)
	27	1 voy. stères, stalles et tôle (2 paires 2 personnes)
		1 voy. planche ouvrier, attelage 1 sac de ciment (3 jours 1 paire
	10	1 voy de gravier avec 2 paires 2 personnes
	11	2 voyages 1000 briques et 2 précintois 2 stalles (2 paires 2 personnes
	12	1 voyage sans de St Castin et du chaux sur les bœuf 2 paires 2 personnes
	13	1 voyage sans de St Castin, chaux, divers ferrure 1 paire 1 personne
	15	1 voy. à table 2 personnes 2 paires ...
	17	2 voyages table 2 personnes 2 paires ...
	18	1 voyage cosbrigieux . 2 paires deux personnes
	20	1 voy. gravier de la tôle et 6 courant, os litceaux
	21	1 voy 12 sacs de ciment et 10 de chaux .
	24	1 voy stères, briques, ciment, bœuferie, 1 paire, 1 personne
	26	1 voy 12 sacs de chaux chez Castel

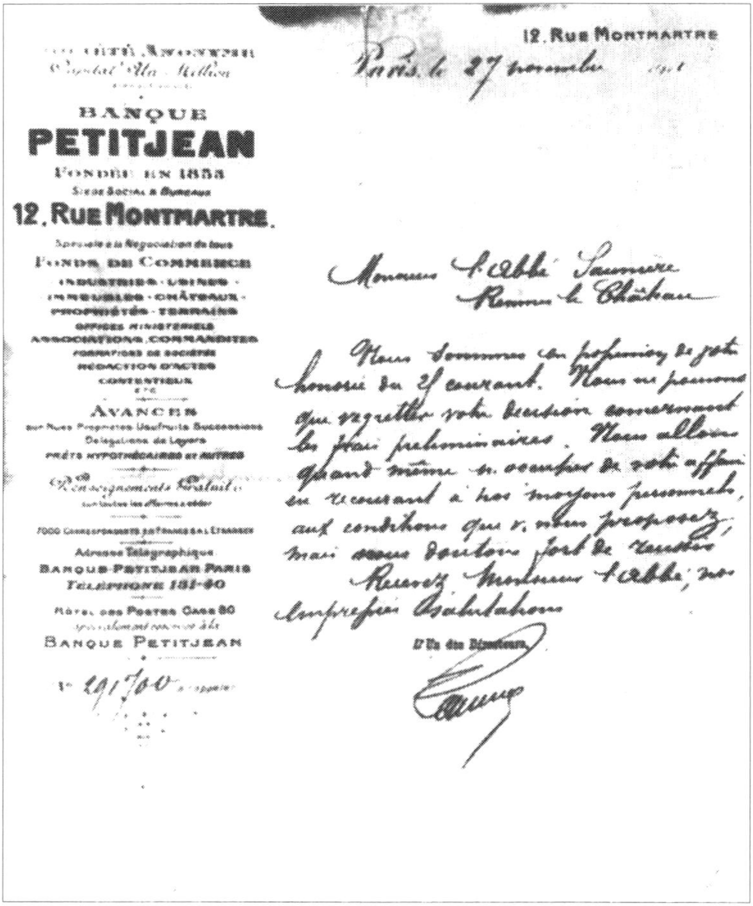

BANQUE
PETITJEAN
FONDÉE EN 1853
12, RUE MONTMARTRE
FONDS DE COMMERCE
INDUSTRIES - USINES -
IMMEUBLES - CHÂTEAUX -
PROPRIÉTÉS - TERRAINS
OFFICES MINISTÉRIELS
ASSOCIATIONS, COMMANDITES
FORMATION DE SOCIÉTÉS
RÉDACTION D'ACTES
CONTENTIEUX
ETC
AVANCES
PRÊTS HYPOTHÉCAIRES ET AUTRES
Renseignements Gratuits
Adresse Télégraphique
BANQUE-PETITJEAN-PARIS
TÉLÉPHONE 151-80
HÔTEL DES POSTES CASE 80
BANQUE PETITJEAN

12, RUE MONTMARTRE

Paris, le 27 novembre

Monsieur l'Abbé Saunière
Rennes le Château

Nous sommes en possession de votre honorée du 25 courant. Nous ne pouvons que regretter votre décision concernant les frais préliminaires. Nous allons quand même nous occuper de votre affaire en recourant à nos moyens personnels, aux conditions que vous nous proposez, mais nous doutons fort de réussir.
Recevez, Monsieur l'Abbé, nos empressées salutations.

P. le Directeur

Dealings with banks

The Bishopric demands explanation of expenditure...

... but Saunière only sends false accounts.

Chapter 3

THE BARBERS OF MIDAS

> "*Where reading is concerned, attention consists in penetrating the sense of words to the profound layers of etymology and the mysteries of utterance. It is the first principle in the art of reading. The second resides in memory: one must preserve the discovered meanings in order to associate them according to their logic, letting slip none of the inherent possibilities of reasoning which they contain.*"
>
> Dominique AUBIER
>
> *(Don Quichotte, prophète d'Israël)*
> *(Don Quixote, Prophet of Israel*)

> "*Language is the place of revelations, that part of space where truth manifests and expresses itself.*"
>
> Michel FOUCAULT
>
> *(Les Mots et les Choses)*
> *(Words and Things)*

Weighty discoveries always create a profound change in the world-view of those who make them. And all the more, since the discoverer of an astonishing find, if he cannot reveal it, will be captive to an almost unbearable contradiction... between pride, which will urge him to reveal it and fear, which constrains him to remain silent. One may imagine him, with a life-long obsession with what he has seen... which may perhaps have been frightening... but of which he can speak to no-one. The age-old fable of the Barber of Midas gives us an idea of this dilemma. Having discovered that his lord conceals beneath his cap the ears of an ass, he digs a hole to whisper his secret to the earth and then hastily covers it again. But there, the rushes grew and with the slightest breath, spread wide his indiscretion. For such a man, the only way would thus be to speak, but to take care that he cannot be understood, or to make himself understood while watching his tongue. But to achieve this, ordinary language is of no use. So he will have to invent another language... create an ocean into which he can safely toss his message-in-a-bottle. Which is to say — if he does not already know of it — he must reinvent hermetism.

Such might well have been the singular game of wit employed by the successive holders of the secret of Rennes — and century after century, inspired them to construct a fantastic puzzle, in face of which the well-known saying of André Breton: "The imaginary is that which tends to become real", is but a feeble expression.

At least, this was the first idea which came to me when, on a day in February 1964, in Paris, after a great deal of prevarication, I was entrusted with two documents which, I was assured, would put me on the track of what might prove to be the most fantastic affair.

These were copies of two of the parchments found by Bérenger Saunière beneath the high altar of his church. On them, one can read two passages from the Gospels, written in Latin. The first, taken from John (ch XII, v 1-12) is the account of the visit of Christ to the house of Lazarus, Martha and Mary of Magdala in Bethany (Manuscript I).

The second has the parable of the ears of corn, rubbed on the Sabbath day (Manuscript II). Here, as one can see, the writer has complicated matters, as he has combined in a single text the three versions of this episode; those of Luke (ch VI, v 1-5), Matthew (ch XII, v 1-8) and Mark (ch II, v 23-28).

I immediately noticed two things: first, despite their archaic style, these documents do not appear to be very old; secondly, both seem to be encrypted. Into the clear text of the first have been inserted one hundred and twenty-eight [51] additional letters which, taken in sequence, make no apparent sense. In the second, one can

---

51   There are, in fact, 140 interpolated letters. (Translator's note)

JESVSEVRGOANTCESEXATPESPASCShAEVENJIThEThqANTAMVRAT
FVERAOTIAZA=VVSMORTVVVS qVEMMSVSCTYTAVITIYESVSFEACERVNT
LAVIEM=TTCAENAPMThTETOMARTHAhMINISTRRAbATCbASARVSO
VEROVNXVSERATTE=ATSCOVMLENTATLVSCVJMMARTALERGOACbCEP
TILKTbRAMYNNGENTTJNARATPFTJTTCIqPRETTOVSTCTVNEXTTPE
APESTERVAETEXTEJRSTTCAYPTIRTSNSVISPEPACSERTPTETAOMbESTM
PLFTIAESTEEXVNGETNTTOAAEREATXALTERGOVRNVMEXAGTSCTPVAL
TSETVTXTVAAXUSCARJORTTSqVIYERATCVhMTRAATTTYRYSqTVAREbOCCVN
bEN VIVMNONXVENŸTTGRECENPATSAENZARŸSETAAATVMESGTE
GENTÉS? ATXINVFEMhOÉCNONqVSTAAEEGAENTSPERRTINEbEAT
AACVTMSEAqVNQFVRELKTETLOVCVIOSHCAbENSECAqVAEMVTTTEbA
NMTVRPOTRAbETEATXTTEJRGOTEShVSSTNEPTLLAMVNTIXAIIEMS
EPVLGTVKAEMSEAESCRVNETILLqVAPAVPJERESENhTMSEMPGEKhA
bEMTTSNObLTTSCVMFMEAVIETMNONSESMPERhAVbEMSCJOGNO
VILTEROTZVKbAMVqLTAEXTMVAACTSTqVTATLOLTCESTXETVENE
ARVNTNONNPROTEPRTESVmETANT=MMSEAVTLVZARVMPVTAER
EhmTqVEMKSVSCTAOVTTAMORRTVTSCPOGTTAVKERVNTAhVTEMP
RVTNCTPEJSSACERCAOTVMVMTETLAZAARVMTNATERFICTRENTq
LVTAMYLVTTPROPqTERILhXVMAbTbGNTCXVGT=AETSNETCRCA
AEbAMTANTESVM

NO ⟨N compass⟩ IS

JÉSV. MEDÈLA. VVLNÉRVM ✠ SPES.VNA. POENITENTIVM.
PER. MAGDALÆNÆ. LACHRYMAS ✠ PECCATA. NOSTRA. DILVAS.

Figure 13.
Manuscrit I

see letters out of alignment, others picked out by a dot, lines of different length, etc. Finally, in both there are hieroglyphic shapes, which could be keys to the interpretation.

In dealing with documents of this sort, one can never be too careful. I have no particular competence in either ancient scripts or coded writing. My first concern, therefore, was to have these manuscripts subjected to a double evaluation, both palaeographic and cryptographic.

I began by having them submitted to M. Debant, a graduate of the School of Palaeography and Director of the Departmental Archives of the Aude, who was kind enough to send me his conclusions in writing. The result was: 1. the documents were not, in fact, very old. 2. They were both written by the same hand. 3. That their creator was skilled in palaeography and mediaeval epigraphy. 4. That he had used his expertise, not to create a forgery... which would not have fooled a specialist... but to attract the reader's attention by means of deliberate anomalies. Some time later, in the course of an interview, M. Debant told me that the documents could not be accurately dated; he could only be certain of one thing: that they did not pre-date the Renaissance.

With the generous assistance of Commandant Lerville, President of the Association of the Military Cipher Reserve, I was able to call upon several specialists in this

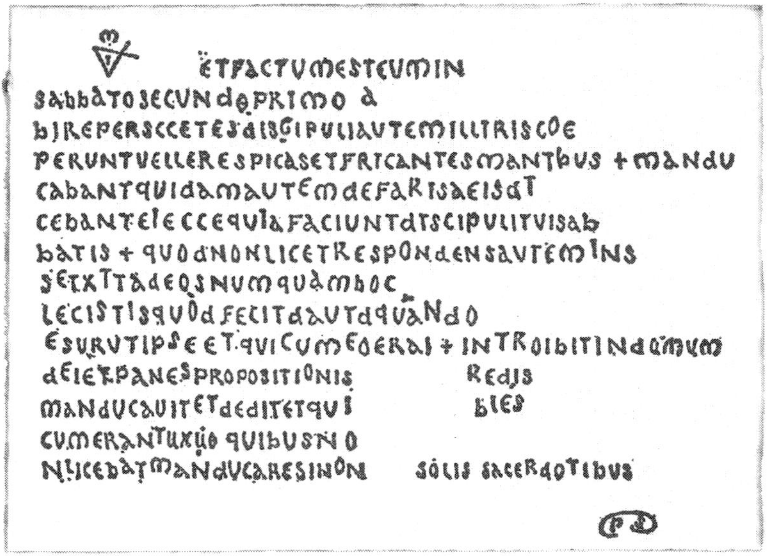

ÉTFACTUMESTCUMIN
sabbatosecundoprimo à
bireperscceresaiscipuliautemilitriscoe
peruntuellerespicasetfricantesmanibus + mandu
cabantquidamautemdefariseisat
cebanteleccequiafaciuntdiscipulituisab
batis + quodnonliceTResponden sautemins
setxttadeqsnumquambic
legistisquodfecitdautdquando
esurutipse et quicumeoerat + introibitindomum
deiexpanesproposicionis   Redis
manducauitetdeditetqui   bles
cumerantuxijo quibusno
Nijcebatmanducaresinon   sóliss acerdotibus

Figure 14.

Manuscrit II

discipline. With the two manuscripts, I also gave them copies of the two tombstones as well as the Coumesourde Stone, with the suggestion that there might be some sort of connection between them. At the end of a highly technical study, the following were their conclusions: 1. the texts had indeed been encoded using a double-keyed substitution cipher and then a transposition cipher which made use of a chess-board. 2. To the cipher, as such, the creator had added rebuses. 3. Errors had been deliberately inserted to thwart attempts at decoding by leading the decipherer onto false trails.

What now remained was to uncover the identity of the Machiavellian author of this brain-teaser. According to Col. Arnaud, Chief of the Army Signals Regiment and eminent cipher-expert, he was, without doubt, "a clergyman, steeped in Scripture and a lover of mystery and the fantastic." Given that one of the manuscripts bears the hieroglyph PS, which figures on the gravestone of the Marquise de Blanchefort one may... and with no great risk of error, believe me... assign to all these texts the same signature, that of the Abbé Bigou. [52]

---

[52]   We would, of course, have hoped to assemble some documentation relating to so singular a character as the Abbé Antoine Bigou. We have searched for them in his native region, Sournia (Pyrénées-Orientales). This is the reply which we received from the Director of Archives of the *Pyrénées-Orientales: "All documents relating to this region were legally removed from the local town-halls by a collector in the XIX*[TH] *century, since when all trace of them has been lost."* (Author's note)

RENNES CELTIQUE.

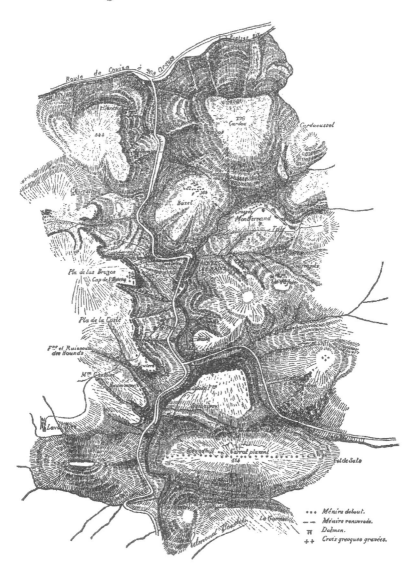

Figure 15.
Henri Boudet's curious work *The True Celtic Tongue and the Cromleck of Rennes-les-Bains* includes a map

But while Antoine Bigou, after all, simply dabbled in the cryptographic art — albeit somewhat strangely... someone who is to come after him is to engage in a truly fantastic undertaking. He will concoct an atlas in the guise of a treatise on linguistics and then go on to fake the entire landscape around Rennes-les-Bains.

On the surface, this person gave the appearance of being quite unremarkable. Henri Boudet was born of a humble family in Quillan in 1837. He was exceptionally intelligent and so was soon noticed by a wealthy ecclesiastic, the Abbé de Cayron, who paid for his education. [53] He entered the church young and in 1872 became curé of Rennes-les-Bains. Poor but openhanded, his flock cherished the memory of him as a saint, others remembered him as a benefactor of the little town. He knew every stone in the region and the Midi's intellectual journals happily published his erudite writings.

Henri Boudet published *La Vraie Langue celtique et le Cromlech de Rennes-les-Bains* (The True Celtic Language and the Cromlech of Rennes-les-Bains) in Carcassonne in 1886. If you read this book a little too quickly, your

---

[53]   The Abbé de Cayron was curé of Saint-Laurent de Cabrerisse (Aude). His obituary, published in *La Semaine Religieuse* (The Religious Weekly) in 1897, gives the following information: "He had rebuilt his church almost completely in fine gothic proportions and apart from what was given to him by the family of Rennes, nobody has ever discovered whence came the funds to pay for such an enormous undertaking." (Author's note)

first impulse will be to consign the author to the category of "literary buffoon". Without batting an eyelid, he claims that the mother tongue of the human race is that of the Celts; that it has remained unchanged until today in the twin languages of English and Occitan, from which, consequently, all others derive... including Hebrew, Basque and Kabylian. [54] The etymological examples which he puts forward in support of this thesis are delectable. The Numidians, for example, would appear to derive their name from the fact that they led their flocks to pasture in "new meads"!

But one soon begins to wonder: with every page packed with so much nonsense, is one not being nudged to read again, but this time between the lines? And this second attempt, if done with care, is most instructive. As the title itself tell us, the etymological fantasies of the author are no more than a cover; his true purpose is geographical. It is the description of a supposed megalithic enclosure of which Rennes-les-Bains is the centre. This purported treatise on linguistics is, moreover, adorned with engravings of menhirs and rocks as well as a detailed map of the area. In addition, on the very first page, Boudet warns us — not without humour: *"The study of the magnificent Celtic megalithic monument of Rennes-les-Bains has led us with certainty to etymological deductions which we consider to be beyond dispute."* This,

---

54   The Kabylian language is spoken by the Berber population of Northern Algeria. (Translator's note)

without further ado, is hinting to the reader that the discussion is going to be geographical, but in a coded language.

In theory, Boudet's coding system is very simple and the author himself points this out quite clearly in the form of a dissertation upon a so-called Punic language, the pure product of his own imagination. He writes: *"Notice how simply the punic language, with its word-play, is able to create proper names of men. Common nouns also offer similar combinations and represent, in a few linked monosyllables, entire phrases which have a rigorous and precise meaning. We shall select a few of these expressions, so that one may see with what admirable care the words — nouns or verbs — are composed."* One can hardly state more clearly that the work is encoded by means of a method very dear to hermeticists: that of punning and wordplay. So the pseudo-linguistic meanderings have no other purpose than to mislead the inattentive reader and to put the discerning reader on his guard. They make a sort of 'framework' allowing the concealment, in a work of three hundred and ten pages, of a few key passages which can be understood either purely phonetically, such as puns or, as in word-play, in divining the true meaning behind the figurative.

These passages are generally indicated by the illogical introduction of the word "key". For example: "Cayrolo", a common place-name in the Land of Oc, comes from *caire* which means a squared stone — in Latin *quadrum.* But Boudet, against all evidence, claims that "Cayrolo" comes from the three English words: *key, ear* and *hole.* This nonsense is only there to give us a signal of the "key passage" which immediately follows: *Cayrolo of the Redones, silo or cave enclosing the precious cereal, is situated to the south of Montferrand, immediately beside the track leading to the stream of La Coume and to the Artigues. The production of corn being extremely abundant, one was obliged to have the help of strangers in these parts in order to harvest more rapidly.* But as is well known, 'corn' is slang for 'gold'. The cave near to Montferrand enclosing the precious cereal is therefore nothing other than the ancient mine situated at this place and mentioned in the report of the Prefect Barante. And the foreign harvesters of days gone by, as the knowledgeable reader can recognise without difficulty, are the German miners and smelters who were brought here by the Templars in the XIITH century.

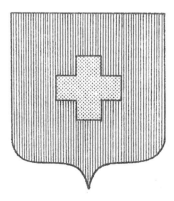

Figure 16.
Arms of Rennes-les-Bains Gules - a gold cross he arms express the belief of thein habitants in the existence of gold ontheir land.

Throughout the book, examples of this kind become more numerous and soon the reader begins to wonder. What the devil is Boudet trying to convey to a *happy few* while keeping the majority in the dark? The answer, surprising as it may seem, is this: it is the secret of a place, with the precautions to be taken in order to reach it and the necessity for silence once the discovery has been made.

As for the place... the book tells us almost all there is to know: that it is only accessible at certain times of the year; that one must go alone and warmly clad; that one must set off at sunrise; that it begins with a difficult climb; that an easier walk follows until one reaches a field, then a fountain, then a sheep-fold with sheep and where one should beware of the biting of ticks; that it is a natural cavern; that one should not proceed without care as the entrance is blocked by a dangerous siphon; that it is risky to illuminate the place; that one's eyes will water there, but one must not rub them; that there is the risk of breaking a leg; that one will come upon a horrifying spectacle, but one may plunder the place; that one will leave with white hair and that it is necessary thereafter to obey the instructions to speak of it only cryptically.

All this is spelled out on pages 120 to 126 of this extraordinary book. Stripped of its verbiage the text, in fact, is the following: *January: bad weather stops the work. February: it is warm enough to ensure the melting of the ice. March: continuous rain turns the terrain into a morass. July: to delay large reunions or meetings. August: the streams cease to flow. September: to wish to go to ground, to shut oneself in caves. October: to hurry on with the work, to wear woollen garments. Sunrise: the man worn down by fatigue. In the morning: to walk with ease. In the evening: to run with haste to the dwelling-place. A field. A spring: to begin to hasten its course. A fountain: to precipitate its course. Cabin: a throng of heads under the same roof; to kill with a pin the disgusting itching insects. House: to meditate. Cellar: part of the house where one may be fuddled by drink. Thunder: to see the lightening above which is sure to cause harm. Darkness: to quieten the humming sounds. The eye closes as if from the effect of a blow. Tears. To refuse that which is necessary. To break a leg. To utter cries of horror. To ransack. To be obliged to have white hair. To have an eye to the instructions: to speak a particular jargon for the outside."*

This laconic but intriguing road-map is only an example of the many hints which cram this book. Only one is missing but, as one can guess, it is the most important. The Abbé Boudet does not tell us where to find the dangerous and fascinating place which he is describing.

There is of course the map, centrepiece of the book, which is no more than a commentary upon it. But we can obviously not expect the author to give us in black and white upon the page the name of a place which he has taken so much care to hide from the majority of his readers.

And in fact, the Abbé Boudet's cartography is no less subtle than his linguistics. He has created a map which is more detailed than the 1:50,000 official ordnance survey though, in certain respects, it remains mute. The points which are not indicated, however, can be located, as they are to be found at the intersections of certain alignments. The elements which make it possible to determine these alignments, as well as numbers relating to longitude, latitude, heights etc., are to be found in the book, though they are scattered and hidden. [55] Finally, these elements also contain dates as the author, using the *cromlech* as a sundial, has fixed his alignments in relation to the shadow cast by the sun upon certain landmarks.

One can see the entire complexity of the system, as well as the main difficulty in setting it up on the terrain. In fact, as each 'unspoken point' is deliberately unmarked on the map, one must, in order to fix them, arrange four precisely chosen markers on the ground. The number of markers necessary for the creation of a complete itinerary is thus quite large. But nature, which here is chaotic and wild in the extreme, is no geometer. There is no providential placing of convenient reference points around Rennes, either in sufficient number or in the required locations.

---

55   Each time, however, a deliberate error has been placed as a signal. Thus, though the book is signed H. Boudet, the map which it contains is signed "Edmond Boudet". (Author's note)

But the Abbé Boudet was not the sort of man to let so small a thing deter him. The landscape didn't suit his plans? Why should that matter? It would not be his plans that he would change, but the landscape.

To complete the strange trail already sketched out by others before him, he untiringly tramped the mountainsides, creating markers wherever they were lacking. Not only did he mark out the Stations of the Cross, he displaced and cut pieces from menhirs, remodelled the shape of his church and went so far as to falsify several tombs in the cemetery of Rennes-les-Bains.

On this eccentric trail, the curious traveller learns with each step some new rudiment of a strange language whose 'words' are sometimes a painting, sometimes a sculpture, sometimes a rock, sometimes even the casting of a shadow.

Dedicated to the Saints Celse and Nazaire, the humble church of Rennes-les-Bains seems at first glance to be not worth attention. The place is, however, of venerable antiquity, as there was already a church there, dedicated to the same saints, in 1162. Should we choose to enter, we are immediately greeted by a painting which is extremely surprising. This was donated at the beginning of the nineteenth century by the Marquis Paul-François-Vincent de Fleury de Blanchefort, who was so interested in the mines on his land. The Son of Man is dead and is lying, with life scarce gone, in a cave through whose entrance a rock is visible. On his left knee, the anonymous painter [56] has skilfully concealed the head of a hare. [57] The left arm of Christ is pointing to a dish on which is lying a sort of ball. Above the dish there is an enormous spider. This painting has much intrigued some treasure-hunters who, even though they have often denied it, are fascinated by the enigma of Rennes: in the autumn of 1966, Mgr Boyard, Vicar-general of the Diocese of Carcassonne and M Descadeillas, curator of the library there, accompanied by a galaxy of sages, made a pilgrimage to view this painting, without being able to fathom it. If only they had thought about Henri Boudet's book … and above all if only they'd brought to this slightly childish joke, the wit which allows one, without false modesty, to appreciate the playing with words — even though it be a little too simplistic. If such had been their humour and if they had known a little of the local topography, the bizarre painting would have spelled out its message for them: Rennes, which was once called Règnes, is flanked to the west and south-west by a plateau from which flows the stream called *l'Homme Mort* (the Dead Man). The painter's rebus can now be read quite easily:

---

56   It is, in fact, a reversed mirror-image of a painting by Van Dyke which is in the museum at Anvers. Some see here a play with words, as Anvers gives the sound of '*envers*' — "back-to-front". (Translator's note)

57   It is possible to "see" another 'hare's head' on Christ's right knee. There is a third, which is clearer, in the flagrant distortion of the anatomy in Christ's right arm-pit! (Translator's note)

A Règnes (araigne) près du bras de l'Homme Mort qui se dirige vers le plateau, gît le lièvre.

At Règnes near to the arm of the Dead Man which is pointing towards the dish, the hare is lying. [58]

On entering the church one sees on the right a wrought-iron Cross decorated with rosettes, at the centre of which is something very unusual... not Christ, but a Virgin and Child. On its base is the following inscription:

IN HOC SIGNO VINCES
DOMINO VIE RECTORE
PETRUS DELMAS FECIT
1856

With the knowledge that, hereabouts, crosses have been used as markers, let us examine this one more closely. Adorned with roses, it is first of all making reference to the allusive arms of the person who erected it and had the inscription carved. With no disrespect

---

58   Though relatively simple in French, the word-play is lost in translation. 1: The French word for spider is *araignée*. Hence — *A Règnes*, 'At Rennes'. 2: *Plateau* in French also means 'dish'. 3: The verb *gésir*, which I have translated as 'to lie' is used only in certain limited ways. It is most commonly encountered in cemeteries as in: '*Ci git...*' "Here lies...". The same verb is also used to describe a hare hiding in its holt or... more appositely... a treasure lurking in its hiding place. (Translator's note)

intended toward the place, perhaps we may begin to hum the words of a song made popular by Gilbert Bécaud:

> *I've written these few lines*
> *To give you a sign:*
> *What's important is the rose, believe me.* [59]

What catches the eye in the inscription is the phrase DOMINO VIE RECTORE. Word for word, this translates as "To Seigneur Vié, Rector" or "Erected when Seigneur Vié was Rector". And in fact, at the time it was erected, the priest of Rennes-les-Bains was a man called Jean Vié. Now, it is hardly usual for a Cross to be dedicated to a priest — even less so if he is still living. And even less usual yet, in the Land of Oc, that this curé should be called Rector, as he might be in Brittany. Finally, it is most improbable that he would have the title 'Seigneur' bestowed upon him. Sufficient anomalies to make us suspect a double meaning. Indeed, one need only speak the phrase aloud for the second meaning to appear: DOMINO VIAE RECTORE, means "To the master who shows the way".

To discover this *via* which, by a feeble play with words, Master Vié is going to show us, it is enough to follow the simple instruction IN HOC SIGNO VINCES. We must make the sign

---

59   The author's word-play is only evident in the French. The sound of the last line: *L'important, c'est la rose crois-moi*, gives "Rose-Croix". Hence, "What is important is the Rose-Cross." (Translator's note)

of the Cross as every one of the faithful does instinctively when, like us, he finds himself in front of a *calvaire*. That is we must trace the shape of a figure 4.

Here, facing the Cross, West is before us, East behind. To make the Sign of the Cross we must therefore: 1 — trace a line east-west; 2 — then obliquely at 45° to our left towards the south-east; 3 — turn again through 45°, which will turn us towards the north-east.

In doing this we realise that, on the ground, each one of the three legs of the "sign of the cross" or if you prefer, of the 4, is marked by monuments which are as curious as they are distinctive. The first leg (east-west) pin-points successively a lime-tree and a tomb in the cemetery, the *calvaire* "DOMINO VIE RECTORE" and far off, hidden from view by the contours of the landscape, a stone cross set up in open country. The second leg (north-west — south-east) takes us from the *calvaire* to another tomb. Finally, the third leg (south-north) takes us from this tomb to the painting of the "Christ of the Hare" and from there to a stone head set into the wall of the presbytery. On the ground, it is not possible to follow in order the shape of the figure 4, as several walls block the way. Not having the ability to pass through walls, let us do it with map and compass.

Starting from the lime-tree, we must face to the west. In front of us is a strange tomb. On it we read:

Here lies
Jean VIE
Born in1808
Named Curé in 1840
Died IST 7bre 1872
Pray for him

So here he is again, our Vié, who must show us the way! What immediately stands out is the quite surprising manner in which "1ST September" is written, which emphasises the number 17. Are we again to use 'chance' as an explanation? No ... for Jean Vié — (we have taken the trouble to check this in the Registry) — did not die on the 1$_{ST}$ September!

There can be only one solution... to which someone seems unquestionably to be wishing to accustom us... that of rebus and word-play. The writer has cleverly suggested to us a date — the date which we have already seen on the enigmatic tomb of the Marquise de Blanchefort and which we are soon going to find in many places and in many forms: 17TH January. [60]

To the left of the tomb of "Jean Vié" we see another tomb, erected by the Abbé Boudet to hold the remains of his mother and his sister. It is crowned by a cross whose upper and two side arms end in arrows, inviting us to look to the front, then left and then right. Standing directly

---

60   Here again, the simple word-play is lost in translation. "January" in French is '*janvier*' — which gives exactly the sound of '*JEAN VIE*'. (Translator's note)

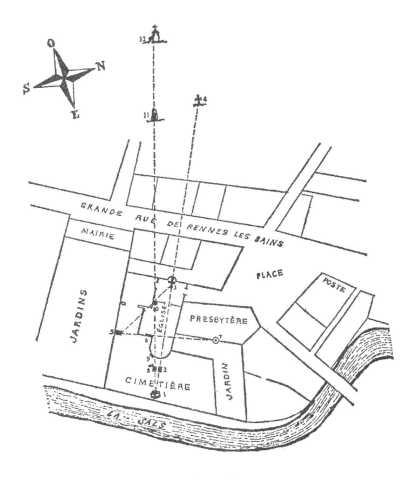

Figure 17.

1	The lime tree
2	Vié Tomb
3	The wayside cross showing the way
4	Stone Cross
5	Second Fleury Tomb
6	Painting
7	Head of Dagobert (also called 'of the Saviour')
8	Boudet Tomb and the first Fleury Tomb
9	Grill
10	Ball
11	Decapitated menhir of le cap de l'Ome (the Man's Head)
12	Church of Rennes-le-Château

Plan of the church and cemetery of Rennes-les-Bains:
"the Sign of the Cross".

in front of the tomb and looking upwards, we can see in perfect alignment to the west: the window of the church behind a metal grill; then, on the church roof an obelisk surmounted by a ball; and finally, on the mountain, the decapitated menhir *le Cap de l'Homme,* 'the Man's Head'. Far off on the same alignment, but hidden from view by the relief, is the church of Rennes-le-Château.

To the left of the Boudet tomb there is another tomb: that of Paul-Urbain de Fleury, grandson of François and Marie d'Hautpoul-Blanchefort and son of the donor of the rebus painting. This tomb is extremely curious as, though one may live a double life, it is rare for someone to have a double tomb and even more rare to have a double birth and a double death. This, however, if we are to believe what is before our eyes, is what happened to this gentleman.

A first gravestone indicates:

CI GIT PA	CI GIT PA
UL URBAIN	UL URBAIN
DE FLEURY	DE FLEURY
BORN THE 3 MAY	DIED THE
1776	7 AUGUST
	1836

On the other hand, a little further off, on the right, a second stone states:

HE PASSED ON IN DOING GOOD
Transferred remains
of Paul-Urbain Comte de FLEURY
died 7TH August 1856
at the age of 60 years

If Paul-Urbain died in 1856 at the age of sixty years, as the second stone states, he could not have been born in 1776 as is affirmed by the first, but in 1796. If he were born in 1776 as the first stone would have it then, when he died in 1856, he was not, as the second stone says, sixty, but eighty years old.

In fact, Paul-Urbain de Fleury was not born in 1776, nor in 1796, but in 1778. Double tombstone, double inscription on the first, double dates. By this insistence, are we to understand that Paul-Urbain, apart from his normal birth and death, experienced a symbolic death and rebirth... the death and rebirth of initiation? And that he then "passed on in doing good" as is required of the Adept? Are we being told that something belonging to the Fleurys has been "transferred" and that we must interpret the false dates as numerical indications?

This would be quite in the style of those who have been painting, carving or writing in Rennes. But surely common sense warns us against such dubious interpretations? Should we not attribute these errors simply to carelessness? This last solution would seem to be the most reasonable... if we had not already examined the tomb on the right.

I have been told, condescendingly, by many an academic that "The Abbé Boudet's book is pure fantasy and should be held in scant regard." However, it should be said that not everyone is of this opinion. Nowadays, in fact, copies of this book can nowhere be found, other than by some miraculous chance. The copy to be found in the library at Carcassonne and which is never, on any condition, loaned out, has been read so much that it is falling to pieces. At the National Library in Paris, it is indeed listed in the catalogue, but you will not be able to read it: it has been stolen. There are still, however, a few very private societies who carefully guard copies on their shelves. [61]

$$*$$
$$* \; *$$

As the Abbé Boudet's alignments, so ingeniously devised, encourage us to do, let us leave Rennes-le-Château. There is only one route to be taken, the Couiza road. [62] In this little town, let us take a look at the war memorial which is to be found, rather unusually, inside the church. Surprisingly, we shall find the same rebus as that on the bizarre 'Descent from the

---

61   Boudet's book has since appeared in several editions and has been translated. (Translator's note)

62   This is not quite correct. Apart from the Couiza road, there is also a road which passes through les Maurines. (Editor's note)

Cross': here, again, the arm of the dead man is pointing to a stone, round as a loaf of bread. Unquestionably, something is being emphasised, even stressed. [63]

At Rennes-le-Château, Bérenger Saunière's buildings and more particularly the strange and disquieting figures with which, like an illusionist, he has peopled his church, overpower the atmosphere of the little village. Here, everything seems to have been arranged with a maniacal attention to detail in order to hint at a mystery and to arouse revulsion in face of it.

Is this place accursed? By whom? When? Why? Are we to take literally the warning which is given us in Latin upon the porch of St Mary Magdalene... *Terribilis est locus iste*? The questions are futile, even childish, but for all that, they float to the surface.

But we may as well ignore the bad taste of all this as Bérenger did not, in fact, spend a fortune on reshaping and decorating his church for aesthetic reasons. Faithful disciple of the Abbé Boudet, what he has bequeathed us in the guise of pious iconography is a trail, a model, which cleverly refers to places he has explored and whose secret he has dragged from them.

---

63   This very strange monument merits a thorough examination. The soldier, one hand on his heart and left knee uncovered, is shown in the traditional pose of the initiate. Draped by the flag of France is a dead tree with a single living branch. An angel, tied to an anchor, representing faith, is crowning him. (Author's Note)

To do this he has used a language of metaphor and allegory which says nothing to the stranger, but is easily read by someone who is familiar with the story of Rennes and with the names of places thereabout. And so his church cannot fail to remind us of the well-known story by Edgar Allan Poe, in which the letter cannot be found because it is all too visible. [64] But Saunière, perhaps inspired by others, does not stop there. What he wished — and has taken care — to ensure, is that the reading of his cartographic message should evoke, as if in counterpoint, a collection of messages which allow the initiated visitor to discover the declaration of an esoteric faith which marks the whole and sets the authors in their place.

Of this latter aspect we shall speak only in passing. Above all, it is Bérenger's invitation to the journey which interests us.

Every map is the representation of a landscape by means of conventional symbols. In order to read it and thus to be able to orientate oneself upon the land, one must understand the meaning of the symbols. These are as many and as complex as the map is detailed. An Ordnance Survey map says nothing to the uninitiated; learning to read it is a long process — officer cadets have to spend long months at it.

---

64   The Purloined letter (1845). (Translator's note)

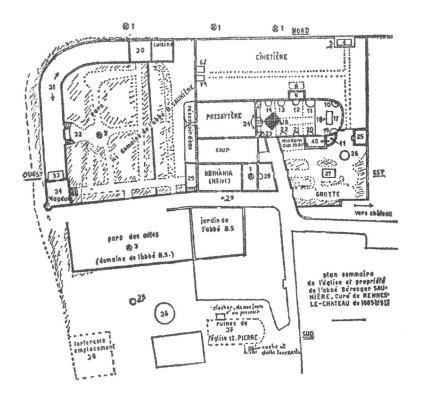

Figure 18.

RENNES-LE-CHÂTEAU

Plan of locations:

1   1964 excavation
2   18 metre-deep excavation
3   17 metre-deep excavation
4   Gravestone erased by B.S.
5   Ossuary
6   Tomb of the Abbé B.S.
7   Tomb of M. Denarnaud
8   Tomb of the Hautpoul-Blanchefort ladies
9   Bell tower
10 St Joseph
11 Pulpit
12 St Antony Hermit
13 St Germaine
14 St John the Baptist
15 Confessional
16 Chess-board
17 Altar
18 Picture of Mary Magdalene
19 Virgin Mary
20 St Antony of Padua
21 St Mary Magdalene
22 St Roch
23 The devil Asmodeus
24 Large picture
25 Temporary resting-place for coffins
26 Ancient baptismal urn
27 Wayside Cross
28 Our Lady of Lourdes
29 The Abbé B.S.'s Chapel
30 Glass house
31 Terrace
32 Staircase and pool
33 Veranda
34 Magdala Tower
35 Ancient blocked well
36 Water tower
37 Ruins of the Church of St Pierre
38 Site of fortress
39 Ancient blocked well
40 The sacristy
41 A tiny secret room

On the French Ordnance Survey map, for example, a rounded hill [65] is represented by concentric hatching. Ask an uninitiated person: "What can you see there?" and the reply will be "Hatching". But if, to indicate this rounded hill one had quite simply drawn a man's or a woman's breast, then even a child of ten would have answered "It's a rounded hill (*un mamelon*)". It is, then, this last method, analogous to that of the map-maker but basically much more simple, which Bérenger Saunière has used. The whole trick is that this will pass unnoticed as hardly anyone would think that religious statues could be concealing cartography. This, however, is the case here. A rather deeper examination will begin to convince us of this.

Here, first of all, in the little garden in front of the church and perched upon the magnificent Visigothic pillar, is a stucco Virgin of Lourdes, distressingly ugly and banal, typical of the thousands which poured out of moulds at this period. One's first reaction is to rush past... but don't even think of it! Let us, rather, read the inscription which Bérenger has had carved on the pillar: "Penitence! Penitence!" These words, which have not been chosen by chance, tell us that this Virgin only has the appearance of being that of Lourdes. For the Virgin of Lourdes said to Bernadette Soubirous, "I am the Immaculate Conception". "Penitence! Penitence!" are the

---

65   The author uses the word '*mamelon*' — which in French means both 'rounded hill' and 'nipple'. (Translator's note)

exact words spoken by another Virgin... the one who, in 1846, appeared, weeping, to two young shepherds at La Salette, near Grenoble. However little we may yet know, this incorrect quotation should put us on our guard. If we have done a little reading, we may remember that in the opening pages of *The Cathedral*, Huysmans makes a contrast between the Virgin of Lourdes and the Virgin of La Salette. The former, he writes, is "the Virgin for everybody, a Virgin of the village altar, a Madonna of the Quartier St Sulpice, a Queen of the street corner". The other is "the Virgin for the few, for the mystics and for the artists". "The Virgin of Lourdes came with a smile and did not prophesy catastrophes"; the Virgin of La Salette, on the other hand, delivered an apocalyptic message. Here, then, we are offered two Marys in one, the one hiding the other. And we remember that not far off, there is a little river called the Sals. La Salette, la Sals: a subtle hint, but unequivocal.

But, with her tears, the Mary of the Salette evokes a third Mary: Mary Magdalene. And there, exactly where the Sals joins the waters of the Blanque, there is a spring called the Spring of the Magdalen. Another allusion to confirm and strengthen the first.

The Virgin of La Salette spoke to the little shepherds of a world war, of earthquakes which would destroy Marseilles, the burning of Paris, the partial depopulation of the globe. It is true that this terrifying story had a *happy ending*: the restoration of the French monarchy to appease forever the wrath of God. This prophesy, at exactly the time that Saunière was employing his talents, aroused in some circles a wave of politico-mystic agitation. The legitimists and even more so the little sects, Naundorffists [66] or the like, obsessed by the age-old theme of "the lost king", found here a confirmation of their hopes. [67] Mingled in with all this was the eternal millenarian dream for, with Péladan, Catholic occultism was *à la mode*; Barrès himself dipped his toe into the waters. So beneath her innocuous exterior, the Virgin of Rennes-le-Château shows us not only the path we must follow, she also shows us an entire ambiance where gilded intrigue and conspiracy mingle with religious speculation. The master builder has thus killed two birds with one stone.

This ambiance shows itself, yet again and yet more clearly, in the porch of the church. There, roses alternate with crosses, a rebus

66   Karl Wilhelm Naundorff (1785?-1845) claimed to be King Louis XVII. (Translator's note)

67   According to the Gospels, Jesus was through his maternal line, descended from David and Solomon and so was, by blood descent, King of the Jews. This encouraged speculation on the possible survival of a privileged human lineage into which the Messiah would be born. These speculations were reinforced by the incontestable ritual analogy between the anointing of Jewish Kings and the rite of anointing established for Clovis. The dogma of the Immaculate Conception, prepared for by the apparition of Lourdes, began subverting speculations upon their origins by raising Mary above the natural order. It is therefore hardly surprising that the politico-mystic sects preferred La Salette to Lourdes. (Author's note)

within the ability of the newcomer: "Rose-Cross". At the bottom, to the right, a stone taken from the old building is decorated with a lily in a circle. This motif, helpfully repeated within, proves that well before Saunière, builders or benefactors of this chapel were making explicit reference to the Cromlech of Rennes-les-Bains, for a cromlech is a circle of stones surrounding a central stone and in the place-names of the region, the word "lily" (*lys*) (from the Latin *lesia*), denotes a standing stone. But it also confirms that they were not unaware of Nostradamus's verse concerning "the ring and the lily".

Once through the door of the church, we are greeted by a statuary group which is, to say the least, surprising. A hideous life-sized devil, carved and painted, supports the Holy Water stoup. He seems to be sitting upon an invisible seat, his right leg twisted and he rests the five fingers of his left hand upon his knee. The thumb and index finger of his right hand form a circle. The knotted muscles of his chest are anatomically 'not quite right': one side is flat and the nipple is nowhere near to being correctly placed. Above the Holy Water stoup which he supports, is a cartouche with the initials B.S., flanked by two heraldic beasts: basilisks. Surmounting all, four angels are making the four gestures of the Sign of the Cross, with the inscription *PAR CE SIGNE TU LE VAINCRAS* (In this sign thou shalt conquer him). We may well feel that this strange and artificial group of ill-assorted elements is a species of hieroglyph.

The lameness of the devil suggests at the same time, his name and what he has come here to do. As is common knowledge, the crippled devil is Asmodeus. And the Bible, as well as the Jewish commentaries know as the Midrash, tell us that it was to him that Solomon entrusted guardianship of the cave which held his treasure. When one day the king was in need of his Seal, the demon refused him access to the cavern. It was only when Solomon had found his ring that he was able to drive Asmodeus out into the desert. And so, in making his devil lame, Bérenger is telling us clearly what subject he wants to talk to us about... the treasure which, as we remember, local legend says is guarded by the devil near to Blanchefort and concerning which the Marquis de Fleury had gone to law, as it was to be found on his land.

If, by any chance, curiosity should take hold on us, we will be shown a precise area for our exploration. In fact, we merely have to utter the names... each detail of the monument is indicating a place in the vicinity. Let us see for ourselves:

The devil seems to be seated: there is a rock called the Devil's Armchair.

Two of his fingers form a circle: there is a spring known as the Spring of the Circle.

One side of his chest is flat: there is, near to the 530 contour-line of the ordnance survey map, a place called the *Pla de la Coste.* [68]

The nipple is out of place: there is a place called the Devil's Breast, mentioned by Catel, on the site of an ancient signal tower... the word for 'breast' (*sein*) is here the corruption of "seing", in Latin *signum.*

The devil is supporting the water stoup with, above, the initials BS: there is a place called "the Holy Water Stoup" and it is located exactly between the rivers Blanque (B) and Sals (S). Bérenger Saunière is here playing cleverly with his own initials.

Finally, *the devil places his five fingers on his knee*: on the rock known as the Bread Rock, there are five hollows suggesting the imprint of five fingers and which is known as the Devil's Hand.

But here Saunière has been more subtle. The rebus is 'layered' and is indicating a date: 'Five' (*cinq*) and 'Knee' (*genou*) effectively give Saint Genou — a saint whose feast day is... the 17TH January!

A glance at the map shows that all these indicated places are approximately oriented to one another on the monument as they are on the ground... so even the most incredulous must grant that there is no question of an accumulation of coincidences.

The device written below the angels:

68   This is yet another play with words. Spoken aloud, the French *can* suggest 'the flat chest'. (Translator's note)

"In this sign thou shalt conquer him", must now be considered. If, as at Rennes-les-Bains, we take the advice which we were given and follow, from the monument in front of us, the route suggested by the sign of the cross... the 4... then we will be led in sequence towards the porch, then, across the tiled floor, towards the font. In addition, we will immediately notice that, everywhere else, the translation of the well-known *"In hoc signo vinces"* is always: "In this sign thou shalt conquer". By adding "him", Saunière is strengthening his hint: what we have to conquer is indeed the devil, the obstacle which is protecting the treasure. This addition also produces a sentence with twenty-two letters, like the phrase "Reddis regis cellis arcis" on the Blanchefort tomb and the phrase "Terribilis est locus iste" on the porch, which are making reference to a cavern which is as mysterious as it is daunting. [69] This number 22 to which our attention is being drawn is not altogether

---

69   Even though it can be translated, albeit a little incoherently, the inscription REDDIS REGIS /CELLIS ARCIS means, if read horizontally, "At Royal Rennes in the caves of the fortress" or, if read vertically, "Thou shalt give back by the caves, thou shalt govern by the coffers". On the porch, with the warning: "This place is terrible", Saunière has carved: "Domus mea orationis vocabitur", "My house shall be called the house of prayer" — the gospel quotation which continues: "But you have made it a den of thieves." Given the language in which we are being addressed, we may suspect an allusion to a subterranean place, a temple or a cavern, difficult of access and containing, like the cavern of Ali Baba's thieves, a precious hoard which requires a 'Sesame' to open it. (Author's note)

without significance. It is the number of letters in the Hebrew alphabet and hence has always attracted many mystic or occult speculations. 22 is, among other things — and the builders of this curious place could not have been unaware of this fact — one of the Arcana of the Tarot — the one called *le Mat.* [70] Is this then a chess-game with the devil which one must win?

If we follow the gaze of the devil, we shall in fact notice that he is staring at the black and white tiles which are arranged to suggest a chess-board of sixty-four squares with its corners oriented toward the cardinal points. In Saunière's time, only this part of the tiling existed: the remainder was added later. On the font, facing the devil, a stucco Jesus is being baptised by St John and he, too, is staring at the chess-board. The two characters — the goat and the scape-goat... the devil, green on a red base and Christ, red on a green base — certainly in opposition, but also complementary — are contemplating an invisible game which neither can play without the other, but to which each proposes a different solution.

Before the font, ritual requires of the faithful another "Sign of the Cross". This will lead us first toward the confessional, above which is an immense tableau — and then towards the altar.

---

70   This card is also known as 'Le Fou', 'The Fool' or 'The Jester'. It can also sometimes be assigned the number '0' — or have no number. (Translator's note)

From here on, being initiated into the allegorical language of Saunière, we have no difficulty in reading upon the confessional another allusion to the tradition of the Gold of Rennes. Adjoining the chess-board, this confessional is adorned with a carved wooden representation of the Good Shepherd bringing home the lost sheep. Certainly, this parable is in its proper place here. But it also reminds us of the young shepherd Paris who, in 1646 it would seem, found the treasure while looking for one of his sheep which had wandered into the depths of a cave. And it is also this of which we think as we read on the front of the presbytery: "The house of the shepherd is the house of all". Indeed, this maxim is obliquely indicating a precise place: the ruins of the house of the shepherd Paris, which can still be seen to the south-east of Rennes-les-Bains, perched like a watch-tower, upon a height.

Directly above the confessional, as if in continuation of the clues, a painted tableau modelled in bas-relief covers the entire upper part of the wall. Here we see Jesus succouring the afflicted, a scene which is in no way out of place in a church. But here, again, it is the details which are enlightening. Jesus is at the summit of a steep, flower-strewn landscape, covered with thick bushes. On this landscape, clearly visible, is a very large purse-shaped bag with a hole torn in it. And the artist has taken care to locate this flowery piece of land. Two stretches of country frame it; on the one to the left, one can identify in the foreground the Bread Rock and on the horizon, the rocks known as the '*Roulers*' (the Rollers) on the Pla de la Coste, as well as the ruins of Blanchefort. On the right is the rock shaped in the form of a gaming-dice, which is at Serbaïrou and in the background, some ruins which seem to be those of Coustaussa. Finally, the cross which crowns the confessional is so placed that we see it at the bottom of the landscape. One cannot imagine a better way to invite us to hunt in the area of Rennes-les-Bains, the thermal spa where the sick are healed; a "flowery landscape"... which is to say, a landscape which once belonged to the Fleury family. [71] A terrain, steep, wooded, marked by a cross and concealing the entrance to an opening which, like a purse, holds something precious.

We shall find a third reference to this underground place beneath the altar, scene of Saunière's first discovery — that of the manuscripts. There, beneath the altar-table, we find a naïve picture to which Saunière attached sufficient importance to have painted it himself. Mary Magdalene is kneeling in a grotto through whose opening one can see the rock of Blanchefort facing the peak of Cardou and also a rock suggestive of a human profile with a large nose. Across her lap she wears a little red heart-shaped apron enclosed between her joined hands, with her fingers, strangely contorted and inter-laced so as to form a grille. At her feet there

---

71   Again, a play with words in French. The family name Fleury also means '*flowery*'. (Translator's note)

is a skull; beside her, an open book marked with two crosses and some illegible writing. In front of her, a crude cross made of two dry branches; from the vertical branch of this cross grows a twig, also dry. The saint's gaze is directed to the centre of the cross. Beneath this picture there is an inscription with the text taken from one of the manuscripts found by Saunière and which is curiously written:

JÉSU.MEDÈLA.VULNÉRUM ⁑ SPES.UNA.PŒNITENTIUM.
PER.MAGDALENÆ.LACRYMAS ⁂ PECCATA.NOSTRA.DILUA

This inscription, being Latin, would not normally have either accents or dots over the *I*s. However, there are four which pick out the syllables JE, DE, NE, NI. Again, this is a rebus which must be read, the spoken French giving the sounds of the words *JAIS* (jet), *DE* (dice), *NEZ* (nose), *NID* (nest), which hide indications of place-names.

JAIS: a jet mine near to Sougraignes, whose entrance can be found under a dolmen marked by Boudet with a cross.

DE: a raised stone in the form of a dice can be found near to Serbaïrou.

NEZ: the rock shaped like a nose in the painting can also be found in the landscape, near to Peyrolles.

NID: the highest point in the area is the kaolin-rich eagle's nest of Cardou. [72]

Note that, as in the '*Christ of the Hare*' of Rennes-les-Bains, the figure in this painting is in a grotto with a specific landscape visible through the entrance. Before some persons unknown partially destroyed it, the rock grotto which Saunière built in the church garden was doubtless a faithful copy of this grotto, whose reality is being so persistently indicated. Here, the placing of the picture below the altar seems to be indicating that the entrance to this grotto will be found beneath the stone roof of a dolmen. [73]

The reference to the place known as the Spring of the Magdalen (*Magdalenae lacrymas*) and yet again to the place known as the Dead Man (the skull), as well as the grille and the 'view', understood in the sense of 'opening' — (or of 'narrow passage') — which, on the ground, could be the "sole hope of the penitent" (*Spes una poenitentium*) who is seeking a way to slip into the cavern... complete the indications of the grouping.

In front of the altar, the faithful must make a third "Sign of the Cross". This leads first in

---

72   In French terminology, a mountain is frequently referred to as a '*nid d'aigle*' — an eagle's nest. (Translator's note)

73   This suggestion is repeated in a curious window in the church which shows the supper at Emmaus, where one can see Magdalene hidden beneath the table. (Author's note)

the direction of the statue of St Antony Hermit. This directs us to another place in the area: the Grotto of the Hermit, whose opening is at the 'Dead Man'. Moreover, the seeker who finds himself here at the right time, or who lives here throughout the year, will see with no surprise that through the window in the opposite wall, the rays of the sun exactly strike the statue on the very day dedicated to St Antony Hermit — the 17TH of January. This once more excludes the possibility of chance.

The last gesture of the Sign of the Cross leads us to the sacristy. There, on the wall, are two inscriptions, separated by a mirror — ANTE MISSAM and POST MISSAM. These remind us that the priest must wash his hands before and after the celebration of the Mass. But, more, we shall find that the cupboard intended for hanging the priest's vestments is deceptive. It has a double back and is hiding a door which leads into a secret room — a small semi-circular structure, dimly lit by a round window. It is in the sacristy, we should remember, that Bérenger would lock himself in the evenings after his long wandering in the mountains bearing his basket. One may well imagine him here, the celebrant in a solitary and secret Mass of gold. Before the round window, hidden behind a black curtain to screen him from inopportune eyes, it is doubtless with respect, with hands cleansed as before approaching the altar, that he worked the noble metal to which Christian ritual reserves the privilege of touching the consecrated bread and wine, the body and blood of Christ, the metal offered by the first of the Magi to the infant Jesus: "Receive O King, gold, the symbol of royalty".

Then, his task finished, the gold hidden, the curtain drawn back, Bérenger had to remove all traces of his work about him, as well as on his hands which he again washed, just as he did after saying Mass. But then, when he crossed the darkened church to return home, the ironic glance of Asmodeus stationed by the porch reminded him that gold is also a vile and sordid metal, inspiring baseness and criminality. Pure in the hand of a Magus, in the hands of Judas it was the wage of treachery. After this 'golden Mass', the curé, captive to his secret, would doubtless find only restless sleep, disturbed by ambition, by remorse and by fear...

In every church there is a sort of labyrinth: the Stations of the Cross. This sequence of images is in fact a pilgrimage for those who cannot visit the Holy Land, the itinerary of a symbolic journey which the faithful are invited to follow on Good Friday at the time when Christ trod the steep road to Golgotha. At each station, the *Stabat Mater* is sung: "Let the wounds of crucifixion, on my heart be borne away."

By its very nature, the Way of the Cross lends itself very well to whatever one may choose, allegorically, to read into it as indications relating to a concrete itinerary. Let us see if this is not the case in the church of Rennes-le-Château.

The term 'Way of the Cross' reminds us first that, on the map as well as on the ground, it is by means of the cross that the Abbé Boudet marked the stages and the sign-posts to an enigmatic journey around Rennes. Red crosses are carved on the rocks at Cugulhou, at the Rollers, at the Man's Head; wayside crosses indicate alignments at Coustaussa, at the bridge over the river Sals, at Jaffus, etc. But in looking carefully at the sequence of pictures before us, we shall see that, true to his method of cartographic imagery, Bérenger Saunière is indeed talking about this particular 'way of the cross'. He warns us at the same time that this path is like the other — apart from the fact that it is underground. The seeker who undertakes it will struggle to the limit of his strength, as did Jesus on the way to Calvary — especially if, like Him, he is carrying a heavy burden. Perhaps his suffering may be even greater, with no Veronica to wipe his brow, no Cyrenean to give him aid. Lastly, so that the clues may be more clear, the statues of the saints, so carefully chosen for their stories, are set between the pictures to underline their meaning.

In order not to weary the reader and because our intention is less to create a detailed inventory than to show the methods used to deliver their message by the master-builders of this most bizarre of places, we shall not make an analysis of every one of the fourteen individual Stations of the Cross. We shall limit ourselves to a few examples which illustrate the methods employed as well as the overall sense. Then, once you are in Bérenger Saunière's church, you will be able, should you feel so inclined, to use your own judgement on those images which, for lack of time, we shall pass over in silence.

St Antony Hermit, whom we have already mentioned, will serve as an example. His association with grottos reminds us that the trail leads underground. Set between the first and the last Station [74], he suggests that the path is circular — that one leaves by the same way that one has entered.

The first of the Stations of the Cross, 'Pilate washes his hands', like the other monuments which we have examined, places the geographic setting in which our quest must be pursued. Immediately one's eye is caught by an unexpected detail: the Procurator of Judaea does not wash his hands in a basin, but in a white platter [75] held by a negro. Blanchefort and Roco Negro: here we find again the topographic rebus very like that which figures in the strange "*Christ of the Hare*" of Rennes-les-Bains. Yet another proof of the intent and the procedure being suggested to us.

Similar indications can be read into Station

---

74   The statue of St Antony Hermit is, in fact, placed between Stations II and III. The statue of St Antony of Padua can be described as being "between the first and the last station". (Translator's note)

75   The word used here for 'platter' is *plateau* — which, in French, conveys a double meaning. Blanchefort is indeed upon its own small 'plateau'. (Translator's note)

VI. Here, a soldier is holding high his shield: one can see a half-hidden tower and a dome: Veronica proffers the cloth [76] to Jesus while Simon-Peter [77] is watching the scene. This group shows us precisely how to orient ourselves on the ground in the form of a complete rebus which we will leave you the pleasure of deciphering for yourself.

If we look carefully at the entire sequence of fourteen stations, we shall notice that each time that the ground is shown, it is in a different way. Sometimes it is white, sometimes black, sometimes mottled; sometimes it is level, sometimes uneven. Nothing can account for the artist making such changes, apart from the need to show us, as if on a model, the sequence of undulations in the terrain which the seeker is to meet on his journey. In the same way, the different positions of Christ — the likeness of the traveller — and those of the secondary characters, suggest the various positions which the seeker is made to adopt by the configuration of the locations. Here one may stand upright, but elsewhere one must bend, kneel or crawl through mud; here one may stay clothed, elsewhere one is obliged to strip, etc.

---

76   The author uses the words "*lin du suaire*" which means 'cloth of the shroud'. This seems to be a co-mingling of the two 'holy cloths'... the Mandylion and the Shroud of Turin. (Translator's note)

77   The author seems to be confusing Simon of Cyrene, who helped Jesus to carry the Cross, with Simon-Peter, the apostle. (Translator's note)

In the third Station for example, Jesus, on his knees, is moving a heavy stone with both hands. This action does not occur in any of the Gospel accounts. It is here simply to indicate a narrow passage in which one can only kneel and where the way is barred by a large stone which must be removed.

In the fourth Station, the traveller may again stand erect but, as the soldier's gesture indicates, he will find nothing ahead of him but a dead-end. It is towards a trickle of water behind him and symbolised by the weeping Magdalen at whom he is looking, which is hinting to us of the route we must follow. Once arrived at this spot, the entrance-way can no longer be seen.

The statue of St Germaine de Pibrac is placed between the third and fourth Stations. [78] This Occitan shepherdess is supposed to have lived at the end of the XVITH century, but her existence is so doubtful that it wasn't until 1867 that she was canonised. It is said that she could only give alms in secret, hid from her wicked step-mother. But she was caught as she was taking bread to the poor and made to open her apron; and on the instant, the bread was changed into roses. It is also said that she would go to pray, far off in the countryside, on her knees in the mud, before a bush and that one day the arm of a little stream miraculously dried up to allow her to pass. Long after her death,

---

78   St Germaine is, in fact, between the fourth and fifth Stations. (Translator's note)

Germaine's body was found to be intact, but afflicted with an infirmity: one of her arms was withered and wasted away.

For the religious historian, this is simply a late copy of the legend of St Roseline de Villeneuve. Here, for the passer-by who pays attention to allegories, Germaine, who tended sheep like Ignace Paris, not only turns us back, with her roses and her bush, to the tableau of the "flowery landscape", but she also repeats the hint of Christ on his knees in the mud. And lastly, she seems to be telling the traveller that he must follow the dried-up arm of a stream.

In the tenth Station, there are several striking details: the traveller is stripped of his garments: as the picture shows, this is because he must descend a steep slope under a waterfall to reach a lower chamber. The pose of the soldier on the right indicates the place where, having reached the spot, he must set his foot. The one on the left, whose head projects out of the frame, the better to attract our attention, is casting dice for the 'coat without seam'. Look at the hand holding the cup, it matches exactly the gesture of Asmodeus of the water stoup. Take note also of the dice, grossly enlarged so that we may read the dots: 5 and 7, [79] which may well be indicating a measure, perhaps the number of steps to be taken.

This Station is separated from the next by

---

[79]   There is also a third dice, showing 3. (Translator's note)

a statue of St Roch. St Roch, (who seems never to have existed), is said to have been born with the mark of a red cross on his chest. A pilgrim, he overcame an epidemic of plague by making the Sign of the Cross. The sickness did not spare him and for the rest of his life he carried a running sore at the top of his thigh. By his name and his legend, this fictional character is most peculiar and very rich in symbolic resonance. His name, Roch, comes from *rubeus* — red, from the allusion to the colour of the cross with which he was marked at birth. Curiously, this was also the "signature" which, it was once claimed, would identify the Merovingian kings at birth and they were thus the Red Line. Here, in a more concrete manner, the saint is indicating at one and the same time, a rock marked with a red cross and a dank entranceway.

These few examples, remember, by no means exhaust the analysis of this church which is unique of its type. We simply pass them on to the reader so that he may become used to this cryptic language... dream-like but, like a dream, coherent and precise. Once familiar with the region and its history and with eye well open to the imagery, the traveller — (perhaps you?) — while reading the details of a mute map, can at the same time also try a little psychoanalysis of Bérenger Saunière and those mysterious people who were inspiring him. Who could they have been? Probably a Rosicrucian sect. The roses and crosses carved on the porch are not the only hints of this. In a curious work, Jacques

Duchaussoy [80], a Rosicrucian writer, states that the Rosicrucians reappear every hundred and eight years. At each appearance they open a tomb containing documents. This information is certainly interesting if linked to the Rennes affair. It was, in fact, in 1783 that the Abbé Bigou created the inscription on the Blanchefort gravestone and concealed the documents in the church. And it is exactly one hundred and eight years later, in 1891, that Bérenger Saunière finds these documents and goes on to open the Blanchefort tomb. Finally, if we add another hundred and eight years to 1891, we arrive at 1999, the last year of the second millennium of our era — a date well-suited for speculation and prophetic claims by those who hold to the theory of cycles. Here no doubt there is a key to explain the interest which esoteric sects have long shown in Rennes, as well as the murky and disturbing atmosphere with which they have managed to surround it.

The traveller will smile, too, at the naïveté of the treasure-hunters who continually invade the church of Rennes-le-Château. Struck by the all-pervading strangeness of its stucco and plaster inhabitants, they have not thought of the rebuses in the *Magasin pittoresque,* [81] as they

---

80   Jacques Duchaussoy: *Bacon, Shakespeare, Saint-Germain*, Paris, La Colombe, 1962. Cf. esp. pp 199-200 and 212-222. (Author's note)
81   The *Magasin pittoresque* was a popular magazine first published in 1833. It continued in various forms until the Second World War. (Translator's note)

should have done, but have turned instead to the automata of Vaucanson [82]. They were in no doubt: these statues were hollow, or tricked-out in some way, or fitted with who knows what kind of secret mechanism! Sounding here, lifting stones there, some even went so far as to tear out the eye of the devil, convinced that it was hiding a push-button which would open some sort of door for them. They very nearly managed to tip over the gaunt faun [83] who is supporting the Holy Water Stoup. They failed to realise that the seeker's tool is neither the pick nor the shovel: it is the head. What they were lacking, too, was just that little touch of craziness which is the only thing to spur the thinking onward — to the wide plains of discovery.

---

[82]   Jacques de Vaucanson (1709-1782), was an inventor and creator of automata. (Translator's note)

[83]   I cannot let pass the extraordinary choice of words which the author here uses to describe the devil of the water stoup. It is strange to equate the Asmodeus figure with a faun (*un faune*) and to refer to him as gaunt or emaciated (*étique*). This is de Sède's subtle nudge to emphasise that he — like Bérenger — is playing with words. "*Faune étique*" gives the sound of "*phonétique*" — phonetic! (Translator's note)

On the mountain, like an observatory, the ruins
of the house of the shepherd Paris.

Rennes-les-Bains: the Christ of the Hare.

The alignment tomb — grille — ball — menhir.

First Fleury tomb

Boudet tomb

Tomb of "Jean Vié"

Second Fleury tomb

Rennes-les-Bains:
"To the Master who shows the way …"

Rennes-les-Bains: head known as St Dagobert.
The skull bears a ritual incision, to prevent the
dead returning.

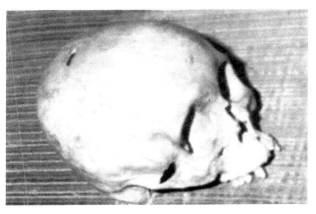

Skull with ritual incision found in the church of
Rennes-le-Château.

Couiza Church:
the dead man points to the stone.

Rennes-le-Château: Porch of the Church of
St Mary Magdalene: "This place is truly terrible".

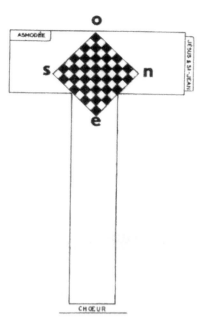

Rennes-le-Château Church: chess-board (original state).

Chess-board (actual state). The broken tile and the two angled
edges define one — and only one — chessboard.

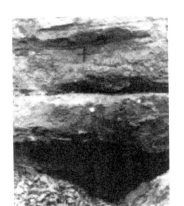

Jet: entrance to the jet mine under a dolmen marked with a cross, near to Sougraine.

Dice: raised stone near to Serbaïrou.

The Spring of the Madeleine.

Church of Rennes-le-Château: the rebus of Madeleine,
the jet, the dice, the nose, the nest.

Church of Rennes-le-Château:
the lost sheep and the Fleury landscape.

On the "Way of the cross". On the Sougraine road is a dolmen closed at one end; clearly visible from this road is a Greek cross deeply carved into the rock on the crest: it measures 35cms (13.75 inches); it is the biggest of the crosses.

Rennes-les-Bains:
Roman Baths (detail).

1

2

3

4

REBUS OF RENNES-LE-CHÂTEAU

The Devil of the Holy Water Stoup

1. The place known as the Holy Water Stoup (the confluence of the river Blanque (B) and the Sals (S).

2. The Pla de la Coste (the rocks known as the Rollers).

3. The fountain of the circle.

4. The Devil's hand.

5. The Devil's armchair.

5

The negro holds a white dish.

Kneel to displace a stone.

High shield. Half tower (*or* half turn). Dome. Veronica with the cloth. Simon is looking.

Remove clothes for a steep descent beneath a waterfall. Place the foot on a precise spot.

Chapter 4

A CERTAIN DANGER

The visit to the Palace of Mirages is ended. We hope now to return to the familiar reality of a calendar, a newspaper, a radio or a television set... the reality of verifiable events, of reporting and on occasion, of the odd fact. But here, in these lost corners of the Razès, we should not rely on this reality to disperse the mirage and bring us reassurance...

Guillaume Servin, agent of the king, murdered in 1340 by the noble counterfeiters of le Bézu, was not the only one to die a violent death for becoming too interested in the gold of Rennes.

At dawn on the 27TH May 1732, Bernard Mongé, the curé of Niort-de-Saux, was found lying dead by his garden gate, with his skull smashed in. His murderer was one François de Montroux and he was none other than the tutor of Marie de Négri d'Ables, future wife of François d'Hautpoul, Marquis de Blanchefort. Immediately after the crime, Montroux, bailiff of the Pays de Sault, left the area and so was not able to be a witness at his pupil's wedding. The motive for this murder was — or at least, seemed to be — pointless. Montroux wanted to assert his rights to the presbytery of Niort-de-Saux, to which he laid claim, but which Mongé would not allow him. After a period of banishment, Montroux returned. As for the disputed presbytery, it was bought by François d'Hautpoul de Blanchefort... with money loaned by his wife's former tutor.

On the morning of All Saints' Day 1897, the Abbé Antoine Gélis, curé of Coustaussa, across the valley from Rennes, was found dead in his presbytery. The *Courrier de l'Aude* — (a newspaper of the time which appeared under the banner borrowed from the Salic Law, [84] "Christ loves the Franks") — reported the crime thus:

"Lying in a pool of blood, which soaks his cassock, the victim has his hands upon his chest with one leg bent up under him. The Abbé Gélis, struck by his murderer with an unspeakable violence and ferocity, has no less than twelve or fourteen dreadful blows to his head, slightly above the nape of his neck. In several places, his skull is shattered, the brains exposed. Three less grave wounds can be seen even upon the

---

84   The Salic Law excluded females from succession (qv Shakespeare's *Henry V,* Act I, sc 2. The Salian Franks were forebears of the Merovingians. (Translator's note)

face of the corpse. The walls and ceiling of the kitchen are stained with large splashes of blood. Though some of the injuries appear to have been made by a blunt instrument, others appear to be slashes. Everything seems to indicate that the victim had put up a desperate fight. Money amounting to fifteen hundred francs was found untouched, though drawers had been opened and cupboards rifled. Why? If it was not to steal money or share certificates or something of value, did the murderer, who had so carefully ferreted through everything, perhaps spirit away some papers? It's an obvious possibility. A few years ago, some masked men had broken into the presbytery. The identity of these criminals has never come to light. Deepest mystery reigns over this awful drama. There are no witnesses, no clues, no trail to follow: the culprit is known to God alone."

The newspaper was not wrong — the crime was never solved. Crowds came to the funeral of the Abbé Gélis. Seen among them were two of the victim's colleagues: the curés of Rennes-les-Bains and Rennes-le-Château, the Abbés Boudet and Saunière.

Today, this affair is so deeply buried in the unconscious, even of the most diligent of the archivists of the diocese of Carcassonne, that we would never have heard of it, had it not been for a chance meeting in 1963, with an old and wise priest, the Abbé Joseph Courtauly, curé of Villarzel-du-Razès. In his latter days, this priest had become very guarded, even going so far as to refuse to open his door for the bishop's vicar-general. Here, as we have tape-recorded them, are the interesting confidences which he imparted to us:

"In 1908, I spent two months with Saunière at Rennes-le-Château. I was barely eighteen years old. It was a beautiful place, but draughty. Saunière was remarkable. With his help, I completed a little painting in the church at Rennes. He paid attention to the slightest detail.

(...) Certainly Boudet signed himself Edmond Boudet, but his name was Jean-Jacques-Henri Boudet. Quite a character... Boudet... He left Rennes-les-Bains in May 1914 — he was having problems with the bishop. They destroyed his manuscripts in front of him — his book "Lazarus" was burned. The Abbé Rescanière, a diocesan missionary, became curé of Rennes-les-Bains in May 1914. He tried to get to the bottom of the Boudet-Saunière affair, but one Monday at about one or two in the morning — it was the first of February 1915 — he had a visit from two people, who have never been traced. Next morning, he was found dead, fully dressed, on the floor. The cause of his death is still a mystery. [85] Boudet is at Axat, in a very low state; he decides to write to the bishop about Rescanière on the 26TH of March 1915, but when the bishop's representative arrives, on Tuesday

---

[85]   Shortly before he died, the Abbé Rescanière was the victim of an attack: he was stabbed. (Author's note)

the 30TH of March 1915 at about eight p.m., the Abbé Boudet has just died, in awful pain. During the day, two men had called on him... There were some strange deaths at this time — like the curé of Coustaussa: he'd been to Rennes-les-Bains to collect some medals. He was stabbed to death. Nobody ever found the murderer or the weapon.

(...) The tombstones of Rennes-le-Château had been copied by Stublein, whose book has been destroyed, though no-one really knows why. I'm probably the only one who has a copy of this book. It was in the Abbé Mocquin's day (...)"

It was at this point in the conversation that the old Abbé Courtauly had a sensational surprise for us, which was at the same time the most solid of proofs.

"Monsieur l'Abbé," we asked, "did the treasure of Rennes really exist?"

Reply: "It's a real treasure. And by the way, I've kept some of Saunière's coins... here's where I keep them."

The old man then took from two small boxes a superb collection of coins and told us:

"Look. These are not from the time of Saint Louis — they're much older — they're not coins of that period. They date from 600 or 700: they're coins of Dagobert. There are even some from the time of the Visigoths. What I have here are two collections from this period. They have the seal of the Merovingians."

We are without doubt the last to interview the aged Abbé about the enigma of Rennes. He died in the following year, in November 1964. [86]

The death of Bérenger Saunière in January '17 in no way put an end to the interest which some people had in this mysterious affair. In fact, since then, the See of Carcassonne has never ceased to watch closely everything which has happened at Rennes-le-Château. Most notably, it has constantly sought to acquire, either directly or through intermediaries, the properties which Bérenger left to his house-keeper Marie Denarnaud. She, however, would never consider parting with them. The hope remained that, as she grew older, she might reconsider.

In 1945, Marie Denarnaud is seventy-seven and it so happens that one of her distant relatives finds himself in a difficult position following the Liberation. His patriotism has been somewhat questionable during the years of the Occupation, and he is interned in a camp in the area. So the Diocese comes up with the idea of a bargain and entrusts a priest — a brilliant member of the Resistance who had been voted into parliament — with the task of bringing it to fruition. If the detainee will convince his relative to hand over the Rennes-le-Château property,

---

86   In his obituary, the *Religious Weekly of the Diocese of Carcassonne* (17 December 1964) said of the Abbé Courtauly: "His colleagues were a little jealous of the contents of his library" and also: "His investigations didn't always get anywhere." (Author's note)

he will be immediately released. The sinner, obviously, is not going to refuse this 'absolution'. But if the cassock-wearing member of parliament had kept his word, he'd be the only one ever to have done so...

The change of bank-notes ordered, without warning, by the Ramadier government, ruined the aged house-keeper. Until then, she had lived for thirty years without problems. In her garden, on the day the measure was introduced, she burned enormous wads of notes which had suddenly become worthless.

Shortly thereafter, Marie Denarnaud leased Bérenger Saunière's *domaine* to an hotelier, Noël Corbu. Filled with good intentions, the new owner decided to look after the old lady and to take good care of her. No sooner had he moved in than the hotelier discovered quite by chance that he was sitting on a treasure. One must smile at the thought of his surprise at this unexpected revelation. Be that as it may, he never doubted it for an instant. Like the children of the old labourer in the *Fables of La Fontaine,* [87] he laboured tirelessly. And how he must have thought it well worth the effort!

---

87   The moral *Fables* of Jean de La Fontaine (1621-1695) are part of every French child's education. '*The labourer and his children*' is the story of an old man who tells his offspring that there is a treasure hidden on their land — but he doesn't know exactly where. When he dies, they dig over every inch and find nothing. But the earth has become more fertile and they have learned that honest toil produces its own treasure. (Translator's note)

True, Marie stayed as silent as the graves which had been effaced in the cemetery — though she did agree to give M. Corbu her old master's few remaining papers. And one day she risked a half-confidence:

The story, as told by the hotelier himself, is that she said: "Before I die, I shall give you a secret which will make you a powerful man..."

On the 29TH of January 1953, Marie Denarnaud was struck down by a cerebral haemorrhage.

"I was at her bedside," Noël Corbu says. "She took my hand, fixed her eyes on me and with a last effort, she tried to keep her promise and tell me. Her bloodless lips moved rapidly. She spoke for a long time, but not one intelligible word came from her paralysed throat."

On the following day, at the age of eighty-five years, Marie Denarnaud was buried beside Bérenger Saunière, taking with her the secret which she alone had shared with him.

M. René Descadeillas, curator of the library of Carcassonne, is an erudite and well-informed man. He has a deep knowledge of the history of the ancient capital of the Razès, on which he has written an important work, which we have had occasion to quote from several times throughout our story. In 1966 we paid him a visit.

"Bérenger Saunière," he told us, "was no more than a vulgar crook and a trickster. He was crafty, but lacked culture... virtually ignorant. As for the source of his wealth — there is no mystery. He managed to get wealthy people to make him gifts, while staying anonymous in order not to upset their heirs. In addition, he took to trafficking in masses. The manuscripts? He didn't find them: he concocted them himself to impress his dupes. As for the decoration of his church, he bought it ready-made, in Paris, near Saint Sulpice."

This conclusion somewhat diminished the convincing effect produced by the visual evidence we had just been looking at: in fact, we had at that very moment just come out of the church of Rennes-le-Château. But the doubts that were growing in us changed to total bafflement when shortly thereafter we learned that the erudite curator, with a few of his friends, had himself undertaken a digging expedition at Rennes-le-Château.

On Saturday 31ST March 1956, M. Descadeillas — curator; M. Malacan — very erudite doctor; M. Brunon — optician; and M. Despeyronat — whose pet foible is dowsing; were busying themselves at Rennes-le-Château. First of all they dug in the church, in front of the high altar where the Knights' Stone had earlier been found and under which Bérenger Saunière had found a little hoard in a pot. Here, the researchers found a human skull bearing an incision in the crown. Dr Malacan, who is taking care of it, was kind enough to allow us to examine and to photograph this skull. It is that of a man and the cut which it bears, regular in form and showing no splintering, seems to be a ritual incision similar to those which are found in the Merovingian cemeteries of Lorraine and Montferrand in the Aude... or on the head of the anthropomorphic menhir of Rennes-les-Bains, known as Saint Dagobert. [88]

The seekers then adjourned to Bérenger Saunière's garden and dug a hole. At a depth of about 1.5 metres they found that somebody had already been there ahead of them. This confirmation was of a slightly disturbing nature. Indeed, their picks had uncovered three decomposing corpses. Fragments of skin, hair, and moustache were still adhering to the bones. On the bodies, knitwear, fragments of clothing. Three men in their mid-thirties. They had been shot. A police captain and a forensic scientist immediately came to examine the bodies. An inquest was carried out by an examining magistrate, but got nowhere. The victims were never identified... the killers never found.

In 1960, a Parisian civil servant takes his turn at Rennes-le-Château. In his pocket, he says, he has a contract duly and properly drawn up, which he has just signed with the diocese of Carcassonne for new excavations to be undertaken — this time in the church. For this, he requests — and is rapidly given — the

---

[88]   A Carolingian document informs us that the skulls of the dead were pierced to prevent them from 'returning'. Geomancers also used pierced skulls to look for treasure. (Author's note)

authorisation of the still jittery municipal council. Both sides agree, however, that the work should be kept quiet. With the help of three friends, our man begins his research. At each session the group lock themselves in the church to prevent interruptions. One evening in the spring of 1960 as he was opening the door to go out, the Parisian seeker sees a dark shape falling towards him. He has barely the time to leap backwards.

"What saved me," he says, "was that, at that moment, the sun was setting in front of me, so I was able to see the shadow of the falling object against the light just in time to avoid it."

It was a wooden beam. It had been propped up so that it would fall as soon as the door was opened. The fortunate man took the hint. He left and never came back.

On the 20ᵀᴴ May 1968, M. Noël Corbu, last owner of the *domaine* and the papers of Bérenger Saunière died violently in a car crash between Castelnaudary and Carcassonne. Is this accident to be linked with another which, on the 20ᵀᴴ February 1967, cost the life of another delver into the mysteries of Rennes... Fakhar Ul Islam, who was found on the railway track near to Melun, fallen from the Paris-Geneva train? The fact remains that M. Corbu was dragged, barely recognisable, from the shapeless wreck of his Renault 16.

A few days later, on the 18ᵀᴴ June 1968, Mgr Boyer, Vicar General of the Diocese of Carcassonne, whom we have seen showing a close interest in the enigma, barely escaped the same fate. Not far from Carcassonne, at a place called the Devil's Bridge, his car crashed into a post. With a broken leg, his chest crushed and a cut to his head, the reverend gentleman only escaped by a miracle.

The Abbé Maurice-René Mazières, curé of Villesèquelande, near Carcassonne is the most affable and level-headed of men. Dark-eyed and honest, broad of face softened by snow-white hair, this former lawyer who came late to the priesthood, is one of the best historians of the Razès and one of the most erudite members of the scholarly Society of Arts and Sciences of Carcassonne. How can he, who knows every stone in the area, not be fascinated by the mysteries of Rennes? On the spur of the moment, one evening I knocked on his door. He threw it wide — having first checked through the peep-hole that we didn't look too disreputable. In his presbytery, austere and bare as a monk's cell, we passed a whole evening talking of the singular story which we have just recounted. He was able to provide many details to point our research in the right direction.

"So..." the Abbé Mazières said, at the end of our long conversation, "you intend to go into all this deeply enough to be able to write an entire book on the affair?"

"That's exactly my intention."

Topping our glasses for the last time with an unforgettable Armagnac, the Abbé Mazières looked me square in the eye and said — quite quietly:

"I can see how much this business interests you — it fascinates me, too. But I must warn you... it is not without a certain danger..."

INDEX OF PRINCIPAL NAMES CITED

BEAUSÉJOUR (Paul-Félix Beurain de). Bishop of Carcassonne from 1902 to 1930.

BIEIL (Jean-François-Victor). Born 19 February 1835 at Boulogne-sur-Gesse (Haute-Garonne), ordained in 1858, director of the Seminary of Saint-Sulpice in 1875, vicar-general of the diocese of Paris, died 23 January 1898 at Salies-du-Salat (Haute-Garonne).

BIGOU (Antoine). Born 18 April 1719 at Sournia. Curé of Rennes-le-Château from 1774 to 1790. Took a restricted oath to the new French Republic on 20 February 1791, which was not accepted. Died 21 March 1794 at Sabadell (Spain).

BIGOU (Jean). Born 1702. Curé of Rennes-le-Château from 1736 to 1774. Died in 1776 at Rennes-le-Château.

BILLARD (Félix-Arsène). Bishop of Carcassonne from 1881 to 1902.

BOUDET (Jean-Jacques-Henri). Born at Quillan (Aude) 16 November 1837. Ordained 25 December 1861. Curé of Rennes-les-Bains from 1872 to 1914. Died 30 March 1915 at Axat (Aude).

CALVÉ (Émma). Born 15 August 1858 at Decazeville

(Aveyron). Died 6 January 1942 at Millau (Aveyron).

CAYRON (Émile-François-Henri-Géraud de). Born 11 December 1807 at Aubin (Aveyron). Ordained 1833. Curé of Saint-Laurent-de-Cabrerisse (Aude). Died 3 January 1897 at Toulouse (Haute-Garonne).

COURTAULY (Guillaume-Jean-Joseph). Born 31 May 1890 at Villarzel-du-Razès (Aude). Ordained 1921. Died 11 November 1964 at Villarzel-du-Razès (Aude).

DENARNAUD (Marie). Born in 1868 at Esperaza (Aude). Died 29 January 1953 at Rennes-le-Château (Aude).

GÉLIS (Jean-Antoine-Maurice). Born 1 April 1827 at Villesèquelande (Aude). Curé of Coustaussa (Aude) in 1857. Died 1 November 1897 at Coustaussa (Aude).

HABSBOURG (Jean-Stéphane de, Count of Méran, Baron de Brandhof). Born in 1867. Married in 1891 to Ladislaja de Lamberg. Died in 1947.

HOFFET (Emile-Henri). Born 11 May 1873 at Schitigheim. Died 3 March 1946 in Paris.

MOCQUIN (Charles-Eugène). Curé of Rennes-le-Château from 1881 to 1884.

RESCANIÈRES (Joseph-Marie-Casimir). Curé of Rennes-les-Bains (Aude) 1914-1915.

SAUNIÈRE (François-Bérenger). Born 11 April 1852 at Montazels (Aude). Ordained 1879. Curé of Rennes-le-Château (Aude) 1 June 1885. Suspended 11 April 1915. Died 22 January 1917 at Rennes-le-Château (Aude).

THE 17 JANUARY

N.B. This page does not appear in the *J'ai Lu edition*.

The insistence which is placed upon the date 17 January found at Rennes-les-Bains and at Rennes-le-Château has encouraged us to make a brief examination of the traditions and characteristic events relating to this date.

Saints celebrated on 17 January:
Saint Sabas
Saint Sulpice
St Antony Hermit
Saint Genou

17 January 1329: Death of St Roseline de Villeneuve at La Celle, near to Arcs sur Argens, in Provence.

17 January 1382: Nicolas Flamel supposedly changed mercury into silver.

17 January 1794: Possible date for the substitution of the Dauphin Louis XVII at the Temple in Paris.

17 January 1851: Satanic manifestation at Cideville.

17 January 1871: The Virgin, holding a red Cross, appeared to young shepherds at Pontmain (Mayenne) to ask that France be consecrated to the Sacred Heart. Consequence: building of the Basilica of Sacré Coeur of Montmartre following a vow of Rohault de Fleury.

17 January 1954: The Pope offers his life "to avert disasters".

It is superfluous to say that we draw no mystic conclusions from this list. It has not prevented others from doing so.

ACKNOWLEDGEMENTS

Enquiries such as that which has been the subject of this book are always difficult and cannot be completed without a great deal of help. We would wish most particularly to thank Colonel Arnaud, Chief of the Army Signals Regiment, M. René Chésa, M. Corbu, M. Jacques Debant, director of the archives of the Aude Department, M. René Descadeillas, curator of the library of Carcassonne, Commandant Edmond Lerville, President of the Association of the Military Cipher Reserve, Dr. Malacan, Count Maraval de Niort, M. the Abbé Maurice-René Mazières, our colleague Pierre Pons, of the *Dépeche du Midi*, M. Vilcoq, cryptologist, as well as those who have wished to remain anonymous but whose information has been no less valuable.

UNEDITED ORIGINAL OPENING
OF CHAPTER 2

En suivant avec nous Bérenger Saunière dans ses folles dépenses, le lecteur n'aura pas manqué de songer qu'il faut les compter en francs-or, et que le franc-or, au cours actuel du "Napoléon", vaut 2,20 de nos francs lourds.

Ainsi, à s'en tenir au compte truqué qu'il présenta à son éveque, Bérenger, de son propre aveu, aurait dépensé, rien que pour ses constructions civiles et les premières réparations faites dans son église, quatre cent vingt-cinq mille de nos francs. Comme le souligne un commentateur, "il s'agit d'une somme considérable pour cette époque" [89]. Or nous savons de façon certaine, par des factures, que ces travaux coûtèrent en réalité un million trente mille francs lourds.

A cela, il faut ajouter l'ensemble de la décoration de l'église. Ici, la plupart des pièces comptables font défaut; mais puisque le calvaire, à lui seul, revint à onze mille francs-or, soit vingt-quatre mille deux cents francs lourds,

---

[89]   René Descadeillas: *Notice sur Rennes-le-Château et l'abbé Saunière (Author's note)*

on peut estimer sans grand risque d'erreur que cette décoration, payée, comme on voit, prodigieusement cher, dut coûter autour de cinq cent mille francs.

Il faut aussi considérer le train fastueux que notre personnage, tenant table ouverte, mena pendant plus de dix ans, entre l'année de sa trouvaille et celle où il eut des ennuis d'argent. A ce train, trois mille francs actuels de dépenses par mois représent une estimation plus que raisonnable: en dix ans, cela fait trois cent soixante mille francs.

Mais nous avons aussi d'excellentes raisons de croire que le curé de Rennes-le-Château remit à Mgr Billard une somme d'un million de francs-or que ce prelat aurait consacré à restaurer le monastère dominicain de Prouilles. Enfin, on peut penser que Bérenger n'aurait pas, à la veille de sa mort subite, signé un devis de huit millions de francs-or s'il n'avait eu aucun moyen de s'acquitter.

Ainsi, entre 1891 et 1917, notre héros aurait disposé, au total, d'une somme variant entre quinze millions de francs-or au minimum et vingt-quatre millions de francs-or au maximum, soit entre un milliard et demi et deux milliards quatre cents millions d'anciens francs!

TRANSLATION:

In following us in our account of Bérenger Saunière's wild spending spree, the reader cannot have failed to consider that one must count it in gold francs and the gold franc in today's valuation of the "Napoleon" is worth 2.20 of our 'heavy francs'.

If one accepts the amount given in the 'fiddled' accounts which he sent to his bishop, Bérenger admitted to having spent, on the building works and the first repairs of the church alone, four hundred and twenty five thousand of our francs. As one commentator has remarked, "it was certainly a considerable sum for the time" [90]. But we know without question, from invoices, that these works in fact cost one million and thirty thousand heavy francs.

To this must be added the whole of the decoration of the church. Here, most of the bills are missing. But as the Calvaire alone came to eleven thousand gold francs, or twenty-four thousand, two hundred heavy francs one may estimate without too much risk of error, that this prodigiously expensive decoration must have cost about five hundred thousand francs.

---

90   René Descadeillas: *Notice sur Rennes-le-Château et l'abbé Saunière (Author's note)*

One must also take into consideration the sumptuous life-style of our man, keeping 'open house', as he did, for more than ten years, between the year of his discovery and his first money problems. To keep this up, three thousand of today's francs per month would seem a perfectly reasonable estimate which, in ten years, amounts to three hundred and sixty thousand francs.

But we also have very good reason to believe that the curé of Rennes-le-Château passed over to Mgr Billard the sum of one million gold francs which the bishop used for the restoration of the Dominican monastery of Prouilles. Lastly, one must think that Bérenger would not, just before his sudden death, have signed a contract for eight million gold francs if he did not have the means to settle it.

Thus, between 1891 and 1917, our hero would have got through, in total, an amount of something between a minimum of fifteen million and a maximum of twenty four million gold francs, or between one thousand five hundred millions and two thousand four hundred millions of old francs!

TABLE OF CONTENTS

1. The devil in the holy water stoup.................11

2. The gold of rennes......................................57

3. The barbers of midas................................131

4. A certain danger.......................................197

Les Editions de l'Œil du Sphinx

If you wish to receive our catalog ans be informed of our new
publications, please send your contact to:

Editions de l'Œil du Sphinx
36-42 rue de la Villette
75019 Paris

www.oeildusphinx.com
www.boutique.oeildusphinx.com

Tel: (+33)9 75 32 33 55
Fax: (+33)1 42 01 05 38
ods@oeildusphinx.com

Made in the USA
Columbia, SC
17 September 2017